why the people

the case for DEMOCRACY

written by Beka Feathers
art by Ally Shwed
color by Gerardo Alba

First Second
NEW YORK

For Chelsea, who sat through
all the brainstorms

GATE 24
FLIGHT 2042
DELAYED
SCHEDULED 4:50

SEVENTY-FIVE PERCENT OF THE AMERICAN PEOPLE SUPPORT THIS BILL. IF YOU OPPOSE IT, YOU'RE AGAINST DEMOCRACY!
PEOPLE DON'T UNDERSTAND THIS BILL PUTS US ON THE FAST TRACK TO SOCIALISM!

WE'RE TURNING INTO A SOCIALIST COUNTRY. I NEVER THOUGHT I'D SEE THE END OF DEMOCRACY.
ALL THESE LEFTIES WANT TO DESTROY AMERICA.

WHOA, THERE'S NOTHING WRONG WITH SOCIALISM!
LOOK AT NORWAY! THINGS ARE PRETTY GOOD THERE.
SOCIALISM IS COMMUNISM! YOU WANT TO LIVE UNDER STALIN?
WOW, YOU CAN'T EVEN FLY HOME FOR THANKSGIVING ANYMORE WITHOUT DESTROYING THE COUNTRY.

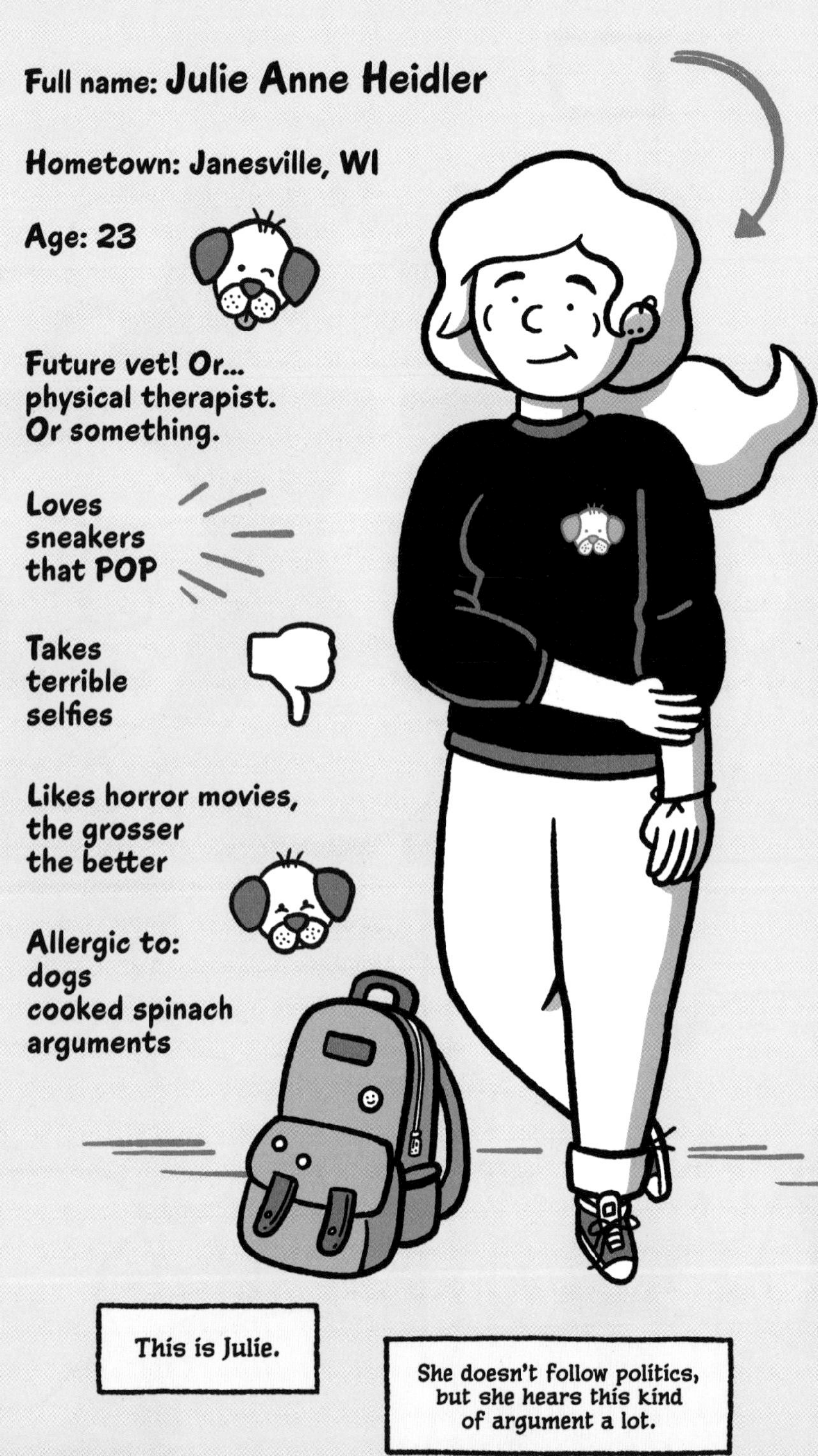
Full name: Julie Anne Heidler
Hometown: Janesville, WI
Age: 23
Future vet! Or...
physical therapist.
Or something.
Loves
sneakers
that POP
Takes
terrible
selfies
Likes horror movies,
the grosser
the better
Allergic to:
dogs
cooked spinach
arguments
This is Julie.
She doesn't follow politics,
but she hears this kind
of argument a lot.

AMERICA BELONGS TO CORPORATIONS, NOT THE PEOPLE!
WE'RE LOSING OUR IDENTITY!
IF YOU DON'T LOVE AMERICA, YOU CAN LEAVE!
Mostly, she just finds it confusing.

EVERYONE SAYS ***DEMOCRACY*** IS THE BEST AND IT'LL BE REALLY BAD IF WE DON'T HAVE ONE ANYMORE...
BUT DO THEY KNOW WHAT THEY'RE TALKING ABOUT?

After all, there are many different kinds of governments.
THERE ARE? I MEAN, I GUESS THERE'S...
COMMUNISM? AND...
DICTATORS?
WAIT, ARE THOSE THE SAME THING?

It's confusing, for sure.
OH, KINGS! KINGS AND QUEENS!

But what are the differences between them?
And how do we choose?
UM...ASK HER?

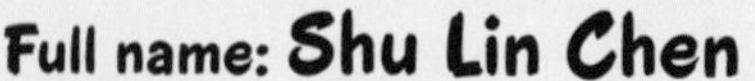

陈淑琳

Hometown: San Jose, CA

Age: 43

Works for the
Santa Clara Valley
Water District

Has two teenage
sons who won't
stop sending
her emojis

Amateur nature
photographer

Likes beach-combing,
hates crossing bridges

Favorite food:
spicy, spicy
pickled peppers

This is Lin.

She has plenty going on
without thinking about
politics all the time.

Her mom and aunts and uncle came to the U.S. from Shanghai in the 1980s.
They're always saying things like:
GOVERNMENTS ARE ALL THE SAME EVERYWHERE: *CORRUPT!*

But also:
PEOPLE IN THIS COUNTRY DON'T KNOW HOW MUCH POWER THEY HAVE.
HERE, VOTERS CAN MAKE OFFICIALS PAY FOR THEIR CORRUPT BEHAVIOR!

EVERYONE ALWAYS HAS AN *OPINION*. AND WHERE THERE'S AN OPINION, THERE'S AN *ARGUMENT*.
But still she wonders: If all governments are the same, why did her family take a chance coming here?

Just like Julie wonders: Is America really that special?
WHAT MAKES IT THAT WAY? WHAT IF IT'S NOT?

Departures

6:45	**MONARCHY**	21
6:50	SALT LAKE CITY	35
6:55	**THEOCRACY**	13
7:05	**ARISTOCRACY**	6
7:10	MINNEAPOLIS	11
7:25	GREEN BAY	34
7:40	**OLIGARCHY**	20
8:00	NEWARK	7
8:05	**ANARCHY**	18
8:20	LOS ANGELES	29

Arrivals

6:40	**AUTOCRACY**	2
6:55	**GERONTOCRACY**	28
7:00	HOUSTON	5
7:05	**CONSTITUTIONAL**	17
7:15	**DEMOCRACY**	30
7:20	PORTLAND	22
7:35	**DICTATORSHIP**	10
7:40	BUFFALO	21
7:50	**AUTHORITARIANISM**	12
8:05	KANSAS CITY	35

THAT'S A LOT OF CHOICES.

IS THERE, LIKE, A PERSONALITY QUIZ, BUT FOR GOVERNMENTS?

What kind of GOVERNMENT are YOU ?

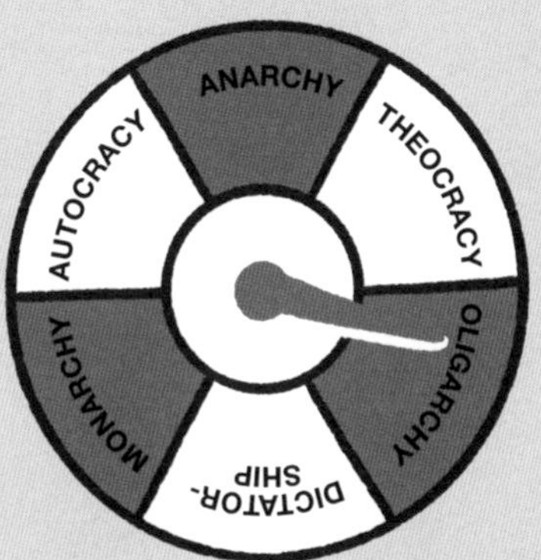

Answer these simple questions and learn the truth about yourself!

1.) Who has the power?

- ☐ One person.
- ☐ A few special people.
- ☐ Anybody who's a citizen, duh.

2.) Where do rulers get their power?

- ☐ Being born into the right family.
- ☐ Wealth.
- ☐ Other people agree to give it to them—you know, voting.
- ☐ Passing a really hard test.
- ☐ Some gods said they should have it.
- ☐ That army over there.

3.) What are the rulers supposed to do with power once they get it?

- ☐ Whatever they want, baby!
- ☐ What the constitution and the laws say they should do.
- ☐ What the people say they should do.
- ☐ What the holy book says they should do.
- ☐ Make themselves and their followers rich.
- ☐ Use it to stay in power.
- ☐ Make sure everyone gets a fair share of everything.
- ☐ Keep the nation safe from enemies.

NEXT

OKAY, SO IN AMERICA CITIZENS HAVE THE *POWER...*
BUT THEY GET THE POWER FROM THE *PEOPLE...*
OR WHAT THE PEOPLE SAY THEY SHOULD DO?
BUT REALLY IT'S A *FEW SPECIAL PEOPLE* LIKE CONGRESS AND THE PRESIDENT.
SO ARE THEY SUPPOSED TO DO WHAT THE CONSTITUTION SAYS?

GATE
AND WHICH ONE IS DEMOCRACY?
WELL ACTUALLY, AMERICA IS A *REPUBLIC!*
I'M EVEN MORE CONFUSED THAN I WAS BEFORE.
R
The truth is, governments are more complicated than a multiple-choice quiz.
Maybe it's better to think of it like a *menu.*
The GOVERNMENT Bistro
WHO has the power
One person........$10
HOW does someone get power
Being born into the right family.....$14
Wealth................$20
WHAT the power is for
Doing what the people ask for
Keeping the nation
Each country combines its options in different ways.
That's how we get different kinds of governments.
CAN I GET THE MONARCHY IN A CONSTITUTIONALISM SAUCE WITH A SIDE OF KEEPING THE COUNTRY SAFE?
GIVE ME A FEW SPECIAL PEOPLE IN CHARGE, BASED ON CITIZEN VOTES, WITH EVERYONE GETTING A FAIR SHARE.
DOES THAT COME WITH A CUP OF SOUP?

Lots of factors affect how a government forms, but ultimately they're designed by people.

Government designers are influenced by the things they see around them.

LIKE... ARTISTS STUDY PERSPECTIVE BY LOOKING AT LANDSCAPES?

OR LIKE THE PEOPLE WHO INVENTED AIRPLANES WERE INSPIRED BY BIRDS?

Early aerospace engineers studied bird wings to understand flight mechanics. Government designers look at how political institutions have—and haven't—worked in other countries and at other times.

Governments are shaped by what their designers have lived through:
I WAS MUCH AN ENEMY TO MONARCHY BEFORE I CAME TO EUROPE.
I AM TEN THOUSAND TIMES MORE SO SINCE I HAVE SEEN WHAT THEY ARE.
THOMAS JEFFERSON
And what they have learned from history:
AMONG THE CONFEDERACIES OF ANTIQUITY, THE MOST CONSIDERABLE WAS THAT OF THE GRECIAN REPUBLICS...
[WHICH] BORE A VERY INSTRUCTIVE ANALOGY TO THE PRESENT CONFEDERATION OF THE AMERICAN STATES.
JAMES MADISON
They're shaped by where they are in the world, including who their allies and neighbors are.
CONGRATULATIONS ON YOUR NEW COUNTRY.
WOULDN'T IT BE GREAT IF IT LOOKED LIKE MINE?
OR MINE?

It makes a huge difference who sits at the table where the government gets designed.
HOW TO MAKE A COUNTRY
And it depends on how much the designers know about their options. Most people have only lived through one or maybe two kinds of governments in their lives.
All of these factors get mixed in with intangible things like who we want to be as a nation and hard realities like who controls the money and the guns.
LIKE, ALL MEN ARE CREATED EQUAL—
—BUT THE SAME MEN CHOSE TO ENSLAVE PEOPLE AND BUILD AN ECONOMY DEPENDENT ON SLAVERY.
MAN AND A BROTHER.
When a government sacrifices its principles to economic and political demands, the results are often devastating.

HOLD ON.
ALL FLYING MACHINES HAVE TO FOLLOW THE FUNDAMENTAL RULES OF PHYSICS OR THEY CRASH. WHAT HAPPENS IF A GOVERNMENT IS IN CONFLICT WITH ITS FUNDAMENTAL PRINCIPLES?
Just because a government starts out one way doesn't mean it has to stay the same forever.
Governments can evolve and change, just like the human beings that design and rely on them.
In fact, they have to.
WHY WOULD THEY CHANGE?
NO MORE
SILENT NO MORE!
NO MORE

Governments—
even nondemocratic ones—
should pay attention to
what their citizens think of them,
because governments have to have
two things if they want to survive.
TAXES?
A CONSTITUTION?
AUTHORITY.
LEGITIMACY.
Governments have ***authority*** when citizens accept that their institutions have the power to make rules, and obey the rules those institutions make.
Authority is what makes you pull over when you hear a siren behind you or pay your taxes even if you'd rather keep that money.

People are more likely to accept the authority of governments when they see them as legitimate. Governments get ***legitimacy*** when they follow their own rules and use their power appropriately.
Legitimacy is why you accept the outcome of an election or court case, even if the results don't go your way.
WHEN PEOPLE DON'T THINK THEIR GOVERNMENT IS LEGITIMATE, THEY'RE MORE LIKELY TO IGNORE LAWS—
—OR TAKE MATTERS INTO THEIR OWN HANDS.
They might engage in civil disobedience or even take violent actions to topple the government.
Governments that abuse their authority tend to lose their legitimacy.
SO NO MATTER WHAT KIND OF GOVERNMENT YOU HAVE, LEGITIMACY IS PRETTY IMPORTANT.
BUT HOW DO WE KNOW IF WE'VE GOT A LEGITIMATE GOVERNMENT?

I GUESS...
I'D HAVE TO TRUST THAT THE PEOPLE IN POWER WERE MAKING DECISIONS THE RIGHT WAY.
WHAT'S THE "RIGHT WAY"?

UM...
I GUESS...
A PROCESS WE CAN ALL UNDERSTAND?
LIKE HOW A BILL BECOMES A LAW. I'D WANT IT TO BE PREDICTABLE.

HM, I SEE WHERE YOU'RE GOING. AND WE'D NEED TO KNOW THE PROCESS WAS BEING FOLLOWED.
TRANSPARENCY ABOUT HOW THE GOVERNMENT IS ACTUALLY WORKING.

YEAH!
AND THE RULES WOULD HAVE TO BE FAIR AND WORK THE SAME FOR EVERYBODY.

ABSOLUTELY.

OKAY, SO, IN OUR OPINION, A LEGITIMATE GOVERNMENT IS...

PREDICTABLE

TRANSPARENT

AND FAIR.

CAN ONLY SOME KINDS OF GOVERNMENT BE LEGITIMATE?

Not at all. Any government can have rules that make it predictable, transparent, and fair.

THAT SOUNDS REAL NICE...

BUT HOW ARE YOU GONNA MAKE POLITICIANS LIVE UP TO THOSE FANCY IDEALS?

HE'S GOT A POINT.

It's true–having rules isn't enough. After all, you might order one kind of government, but get another one.
EXCUSE ME, I ORDERED A COMMUNIST UTOPIA...
...BUT THIS IS A *DICTATORSHIP!*

PLUS YOU GOTTA MAKE SURE THE PEOPLE IN POWER ARE FIXING REGULAR PEOPLE'S PROBLEMS...
NOT JUST THEIR BUDDIES'.

OR GETTING RICH OFF THE REST OF US.

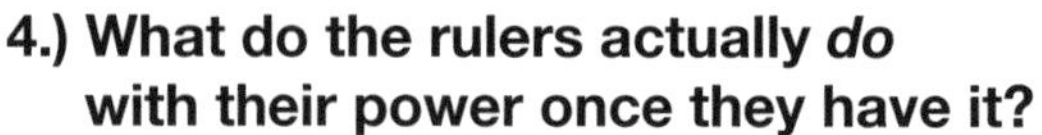

4.) What do the rulers actually *do* with their power once they have it?

In some ways, this is the most important question of all.

Governments tend to prioritize the interests of the people who hold the power.

When one person is in charge, their opinions count more than everyone else's. Their interests tend to get the most attention.

WHAT THIS COUNTRY REALLY NEEDS IS ANOTHER STATUE OF ***ME!***

The more people who have power, the more interests have to be balanced.

WE NEED MORE ROADS!

PEACE NOW!

END THE HOUSING CRISIS!

OUR KIDS NEED BETTER SCHOOLS!

STOP CRIME!

JOBS!

WHO'S MY DOCTOR?

But it can be hard for a really big group of people to decide what to do.

Sometimes it's helpful to limit who makes decisions.

But if only a few people are making decisions, it really matters who they are and how they got there. If they're in charge for life, they might not care what other people need.
JOBS? NO!
CRIME IS MORE IMPORTANT!
WHAT?!
THE PEASANTS ARE RIOTING AGAIN.
THAT'S WHAT YOU GET FOR BEING BORN A PEASANT.
If they took power by force, they might only listen to other strong people.
WE DEMAND JOBS AND DIGNITY!
YOU AND WHOSE ARMY?
If their power comes from wealth, they might only care about profits and protecting themselves and their rich friends.
THIS PETITION SAYS PEOPLE CAN'T AFFORD MEDICINE.
DON'T THEY KNOW THE POINT OF INVESTING IN DRUG RESEARCH IS TO MAKE MONEY OFF IT?
If they're all the same kind of people, they might ignore the needs of people who aren't like them.
BLACK LIVES MATTER
SO, THE THING ABOUT RACIAL PROFILING IS—
NONSENSE! I STAY OUT LATE, AND I'VE NEVER BEEN BOTHERED BY THE POLICE.

Democratic governments almost always promise these things, although they don't always deliver. But these help make a safer, healthier, happier, and more stable country. And governments have more legitimacy and authority when they govern safe, healthy, and happy citizens.

Of course, democracies don't have to look like the American government to give citizens a role in decision-making and the tools to advocate for change.
PLURINATIONALISM
LOCAL ELECTIONS
DEMOCRACY VIA SOCIALISM
DEMOCRACY VIA CAPITALISM
FEDERALISM
TRIBAL COUNCILS
WAIT, THERE ARE DIFFERENT KINDS OF DEMOCRACY, TOO?!
As long as people are making decisions together, the only limits are what they can imagine and what they can agree on.

I'M NEVER GONNA KNOW IF DEMOCRACY IS THE BEST, AM I?
WHY CAN'T YOU BE HAPPY WITH WHAT YOU'VE GOT?

IT DOESN'T SEEM LIKE PEOPLE ARE REALLY *THAT* HAPPY.

MAYBE WE SHOULD FIGURE OUT WHAT DEMOCRACY DOES THAT OTHER KINDS OF GOVERNMENT DON'T.
HOW DO WE DO THAT?

I HAVE AN IDEA.

WHERE'S THAT MENU?

THANK YOU.
The GOVERNMENT Bistro
WHO has the power
HOW does someone get power
WHAT the power is for

WHAT IF WE TAKE THESE ONE AT A TIME?
YES, PLEASE.
The GOVERNMENT Bistro

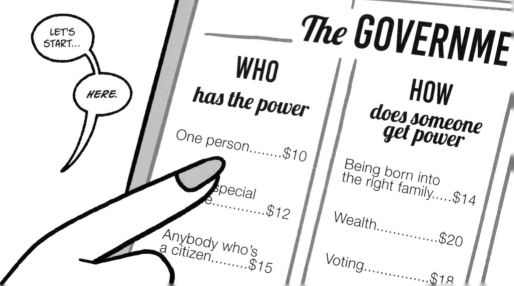

LET'S START...
HERE.
WHO
has the power
One person........$10
special
$12
Anybody who's a citizen.........$15
HOW
does someone get power
Being born into the right family.....$14
Wealth...............$20
Voting

Departures

An airport is a gateway: We pass through it on our way from where we are to where we want to be.

In theory, airports are simple to use:

You arrive with a ticket...

check your bags to your destination...

and use the signs to find your gate.

Follow the steps and you'll get where you want to go.

But it's not usually that easy, is it?

Barriers come up that make it hard to get where you're going.

Designing a government is kind of like trying to travel through the biggest, most complicated airport in the world.
People who thought they agreed on where the government was going will find that they actually have very different ideas.
ENSLAVED BLACK PEOPLE ONLY COUNT AS THREE-FIFTHS OF A PERSON? WHAT HAPPENED TO "ALL MEN ARE CREATED EQUAL"?
WAIT, YOU THOUGHT I MEANT *EVERYBODY?*
It'll turn out that some people only want to get on board if they can be the pilot.
PEOPLE LIKE ME HAVE ALWAYS FLOWN THESE THINGS.
Other people will find barriers that exist only for them.
THIS SEAT'S TAKEN.
AND THIS ONE.
THIS ONE, TOO.

Even if everyone agrees on where they want to go, there might not be a way to get them there.
GAT
14
SORRY, FOLKS...
LOOKS LIKE WE CAN'T AFFORD TO FUEL THE PLANE THIS YEAR.

Sometimes the historical and political baggage we carry weighs too much.
OVER
MASS INCARCERATION
LAND THEFT
CIVIL WAR
SYSTEMIC RACISM
JUSTICE DENIED

Governments and airports aren't exactly the same, of course.

LIVE

BREAKING

DEADLOCK IN SENATE

12:56

Most of the choices you make as an air traveler only affect ***you.***

Governments make choices that affect ***all*** of society.

Choosing a government, like entering an airport, is a departure point—an opportunity to make decisions about where you go and how you get there.

And just like air travel, choosing a government has both obvious and hidden costs, some of which we travelers may not understand for generations.

So we need to think about where we want to go, who we want to bring along, and what we need to take with us.

RULE BY ONE
THIS WAY, I THINK.
The GOVERNMENT Bistro
NOW SERVING LUNCH!

RULE BY ONE MEANS KINGS AND QUEENS, YEAH? LIKE THE QUEEN OF ENGLAND?
OR DICTATORS.
RIGHT. THEM, TOO.

I'VE ALWAYS WONDERED...
WHAT DOES THE QUEEN OF ENGLAND ACTUALLY DO?

type
type
SEARCH

SEARCH
THE QUEEN
WEARS FANCY HATS?

BEING A QUEEN MEANS HAVING POWER, RIGHT?
AND YOU DON'T GET POWER FROM A HAT, EVEN A FANCY ONE.
I GUESS THAT DEPENDS ON WHAT YOU MEAN BY POWER.

HM. I THINK I MEAN THE POWER TO MAKE THE FINAL DECISION ON SOMETHING...
AND THE POWER TO CONTROL WHERE THE MONEY GOES.

APPROVED

WHAT ABOUT YOU?
ME? I DON'T HAVE ANY POWER!

NO, I MEAN, WHAT DO YOU THINK POWER MEANS?
OH, UM, WELL...

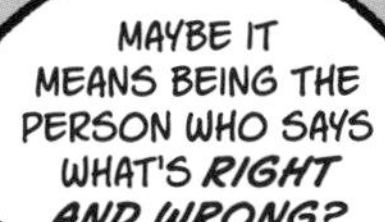
MAYBE IT MEANS BEING THE PERSON WHO SAYS WHAT'S ***RIGHT AND WRONG?***
AND HAVING THE FINAL SAY ABOUT HOW PEOPLE GET ***PUNISHED*** IF THEY BREAK THE RULES?

THAT MAKES SENSE, TOO.
WHEN WE LOOK AT ALL THESE TYPES OF GOVERNMENT, LET'S PAY ATTENTION TO THOSE THINGS.

WHO MAKES THE DECISIONS, WHO CONTROLS THE MONEY, WHO SAYS WHAT'S RIGHT AND WRONG, WHO PUNISHES PEOPLE.
THAT SEEMS LIKE A GOOD STARTING POINT TO ME.

TERMINAL
RULE BY 1
NOW BOARDING
MONARCHY C21
NEXT FLIGHT AT THIS GATE:
DICTATORSHIP
SPEAKING OF DECISIONS, WHERE DID THESE CATEGORIES COME FROM, ANYWAY?
ONE PERSON IN CHARGE, A FEW PEOPLE, EVERYBODY—
WHO DECIDED THOSE WERE THE RULES?
The Greek thinker Aristotle famously organized governments by how many people held power. But every major civilization has had people who think about what government should look like and what it should do.
WITHOUT A GUIDING HAND, PLATO, WE'LL BE OVERRUN WITH VIOLENCE.
EVERYONE WILL TRY TO TAKE WHAT THEY NEED BY FORCE.

This is **Ibn Khaldun,** one of the Islamic world's most important thinkers and historians.

He was born in the fourteenth century and became an important political adviser for rulers across the world. His work took him from what is now Spain to Syria.

PEOPLE IN ANY SOCIAL ORGANIZATION MUST HAVE SOMEONE WHO EXERCISES A RESTRAINING INFLUENCE AND RULES THEM AND TO WHOM RECOURSE MAY BE HAD.

He put what he learned into the **Muqaddimah,** a comprehensive history of empires, economics, and people.

WHO SAYS WHAT'S RIGHT AND WRONG

WHO EXERCISES A RESTRAINING INFLUENCE

WHO MAKES DECISIONS

AND RULES THEM

THAT SOUNDS LIKE WHAT WE WERE JUST TALKING ABOUT.

WHO PUNISHES PEOPLE

TO WHOM RECOURSE MAY BE HAD

PROPHET
LEGISLATOR
SAGE KING LYFE
Philosopher Kings 4-eva
Nearly all early thinkers agreed that the best system was to give ***absolute power*** to an outstandingly virtuous ruler.

WHAT MAKES THIS "VIRTUOUS RULER" SO SPECIAL?
THE TRULY VIRTUOUS RULER UNDERSTANDS HOW TO LIVE IN EXACTLY THE RIGHT WAY TO FOSTER HUMAN EXCELLENCE.
ABU NASR AL-FARABI
Once everyone is living their best life, as it were, society should be peaceful and happy.
THAT SEEMS... UNLIKELY.
Our thinkers expected virtuous rulers to be rare.
So they came up with a lot of ideas about how regular rulers should pursue order and peace.
GOOD GOVERNMENTS
MONARCHY
ARISTOCRACY
POLITY
DEFECTIVE GOVERNMENTS
TYRANNY
OLIGARCHY
SIMPLE DEMOCRACY
NO MATTER WHO IS IN CHARGE, THE LAW SHOULD BE SUPREME!

WHEN THE ***LAW*** IS SUPREME, RULERS GOVERN IN THE INTEREST OF THE COMMUNITY.

BUT WHEN ***RULERS*** ARE SUPREME, THEY ALWAYS END UP GOVERNING FOR THEMSELVES.

YOU'RE COUNTING ON THE ***MASSES*** TO MAKE GOOD LAWS? OKAY. SURE.

SWIPE!

CAN'T RULERS MAKE GOOD LAWS, TOO?

VIRTUOUS ONES CAN!

Chinese thinkers debated whether it was better for rulers to inspire right behavior through strict laws or by setting a good moral example themselves.
A GOOD RULER MUST FOLLOW THE HEARTS OF THE PEOPLE, BUT ALSO SHOW THE WAY TO CERTAIN DEATH.
RULERS GET BETTER RESULTS WHEN THEY RULE THROUGH VIRTUE RATHER THAN FORCE.
A RULER SHOULD GOVERN LIKE THE PARENT OF A FAMILY. TO RULE BY FORCE IS LIKE CLIMBING A TREE IN SEARCH OF A FISH.
CONFUCIUS
MENCIUS
SHANG YANG
GUAN ZHONG
HAN FEI
THE PEOPLE FLOURISH WHEN THE STATE IS STRONG.
YOU WANT TO HELP THE PEOPLE? THEN MAINTAIN LAW AND ORDER!
MAKE THE RULES STRICT, BECAUSE VIRTUOUS RULERS ARE ABOUT AS COMMON AS UNICORNS.

Arab thinkers also spent a lot of time discussing what a ruler should do.
LIVING VIRTUOUSLY MEANS KNOWING YOUR PLACE IN SOCIETY.
ONE OF THE RULER'S MOST IMPORTANT JOBS IS TO MAKE SURE EVERYONE IS IN THEIR PROPER PLACE.
THE RULER'S RESPONSIBILITY IS TO GUIDE, OR PUSH, CITIZENS TOWARD VIRTUOUS LIVING.
IBN SINA
AL-FARABI
AL-SIJISTANI
OF COURSE!
THE RULER IS GOD'S SHADOW ON EARTH. VIRTUOUS CITIZENS LOOK TO THE RULER TO ENFORCE GOD'S LAWS.
THEY'RE AWFULLY CONCERNED WITH *HIERARCHY*...
They weren't alone.
Hindu thinkers agreed that strict social hierarchies were the only way to prevent chaos.
ALL GROUPS HAVE DHARMA TO PERFORM.
THE GOOD KING ENCOURAGES HIS CITIZENS TO PERFORM THEIR RESPONSIBILITIES, NOT THOSE OF ANY OTHER GROUP.
KAUTILYA

WOW, THESE GUYS WERE REALLY OBSESSED WITH BEING VIRTUOUS. AND WITH BEING IN CHARGE.
THESE ARE ALL ABOUT *KINGS*. WHAT ABOUT EVERYBODY ELSE?
PROPHET
KING
LYFE

For political reasons, most of these thinkers focused on governments ruled by one person: ***monarchies*** and ***tyrannies***.
POLITICAL REASONS?

Most of them lived in societies ruled by a single person, usually a man. Kings don't love hearing about the benefits of other people being in charge.
WHAT'S THIS ABOUT HOW SOCIETY WORKS BEST WHEN PEOPLE GOVERN THEMSELVES?
NOT YOUR PEOPLE, YOUR MAJESTY.
OTHER PEOPLE.
TOTALLY DIFFERENT PEOPLE.

These thinkers also lived in times where war was common and peaceful transitions of power were rare.
A STRONG LEADER MEANS WE DON'T HAVE TO DO THIS AGAIN NEXT WEEK!

They didn't always agree on what made a strong ruler...
STANDARDS!
HUMANE GOVERNMENT!
...but they didn't like what happened when too many people thought they were in charge.
"RATIONAL PEOPLE ALREADY KNOW THAT IF EVERYONE WERE A KING, THEY WOULD SEEK TO DESTROY EACH OTHER TO THE VERY LAST PERSON...
AND, IF EVERYONE WERE A SUBJECT, THEY WOULD JUST AS SURELY ALL PERISH."
IBN SINA
SO THEY DECIDED THE BEST WAY TO GET A GOOD GOVERNMENT WAS TO HAVE ONE PERSON TO SAY WHAT IS RIGHT AND WRONG, PUNISH PEOPLE IF THEY BROKE THE RULES...
...AND MAKE DECISIONS ABOUT WHAT THE GOVERNMENT SHOULD DO.
BUT WHAT ABOUT OUR RULES FOR A GOOD GOVERNMENT?

STABILITY FIRST. EVERYTHING COMES FROM STABILITY.

STABILITY BRINGS ORDER...

...AND ORDER BRINGS HAPPINESS!

BREAKING NEWS

LIVE

TO GATES M1-M50

MONARCHY

But, of course, a monarchy is just one road to stability.

TO GATES
M1-M50
MONARCHY
SO WHAT *IS* A MONARCHY, OTHER THAN FANCY HATS?
RESTAURANTS
Monarchy is a system of government where one person is the head of state for life.
Most, but not all, monarchies are hereditary, meaning that the crown passes from the current monarch to a relative, usually one of their children.
WHAT ABOUT COUNTRIES THAT HAVE A KING OR A QUEEN, BUT THEY DON'T MAKE THE LAWS?
ARE THEY STILL MONARCHIES?
There are two main kinds of monarchy: the *absolute monarchy* and the *constitutional monarchy*.

In an ***absolute*** monarchy, the monarch...

...writes the laws and decides when they go into effect. But the laws don't apply to the monarch.
LAW IS SOMETHING THAT HAPPENS TO *OTHER* PEOPLE.

...appoints all the high government officers.
MY DREAM JOB, AT LAST!
JUST REMEMBER, I CAN TAKE THIS AWAY ANYTIME I WANT.

...and controls all the resources of the state.

Land,

natural resources like timber, oil, gems, water, valuable minerals,

human resources,

and, of course, money.

THAT'S A LOT OF WORK FOR ONE PERSON.
YOU'D HAVE TO KNOW SO MUCH STUFF!
ECONOMICS, MILITARY STRATEGY, STUFF ABOUT... MONEY...
FISCAL POLICY.

RIGHT, THAT!
HOW TO WRITE LAWS AND HOW TO MAKE PEOPLE OBEY THEM AND...

IT'S RISKY TO GIVE ONE PERSON SO MUCH POWER.
WHAT IF THE MONARCH IS LAZY? OR SELFISH?
WHAT HAPPENS WHEN THE MONARCH GETS OLD OR SICK?
WHAT IF THE MONARCH CAN'T DECIDE WHAT TO DO? WHO CAN THEY ASK?
...AND HEALTH POLICY AND PROTECTING THE ENVIRONMENT...
...AND WHAT KIDS SHOULD LEARN IN SCHOOL AND HOW TO BUILD ROADS AND BRIDGES...
TRASH
Very few people are qualified to carry this burden.
That's why our thinkers spend so much time on the qualities a good ruler needs, but also emphasized how unlikely it was for one person to have all of those qualities.
!!! ?? ?!
AND IF YOU CAN'T FIND A PERFECT RULER, SUBSTITUTE:
ONE LEARNED PHILOSOPHER, ONE WISE JURIST, AND ONE PROPHET. MIX AND RULE JOINTLY.
It's also why they told rulers to pick good deputies—and to listen to them.
TO FAIL TO HEED YOUR LOYAL MINISTERS WHEN YOU ARE AT FAULT, INSISTING ON HAVING YOUR OWN WAY...
WILL IN TIME DESTROY YOUR GOOD REPUTATION AND MAKE YOU A LAUGHINGSTOCK OF OTHERS.
HAN FEI

WHEW! I'M EXHAUSTED JUST THINKING ABOUT IT.
I DON'T UNDERSTAND WHY ANYBODY WOULD WANT THAT JOB IN THE FIRST PLACE.

THINK OF ALL THE FANCY HATS!
YOU WOULD AGREE TO RUN AN ENTIRE COUNTRY FOR SOME FANCY HATS?
WELL, MAYBE FANCY SNEAKERS.

BUT SERIOUSLY, BEING A KING WAS PRETTY GREAT FOR THE KING, RIGHT?

YOU GOT TO DO WHATEVER YOU WANTED BECAUSE THE LAW DIDN'T APPLY TO YOU.

MY TURN, FOREVER!

PLAYZONE

YOU GOT ALL THE BEST FOOD AND HOUSES. YOU NEVER HAD TO BE COLD OR WORRY ABOUT RENT.

AND IF YOU DIDN'T CARE THAT MUCH ABOUT YOUR SUBJECTS, YOU COULD PRETTY MUCH PLAY ALL THE TIME.

WE WOULDN'T SAY "LIVE LIKE A KING" IF LIVING LIKE A KING WAS BAD, RIGHT?
I ADMIT THERE ARE BENEFITS.
BUT I BET IT'S NOT SO WONDERFUL TO BE A REGULAR PERSON IN A COUNTRY WHERE THE KING SPENDS ALL HIS TIME PLAYING INSTEAD OF SOLVING PROBLEMS.
TRUE.
GOOD THING WE DON'T HAVE ABSOLUTE MONARCHS ANYMORE.
IVALS
DEPARTURES
BAHRAIN
BRUNEI
OMAN
QATAR
SAUDI ARABIA
SWAZILAND / ESWATINI
UNITED ARAB EMIRATES
That's not quite true.

The biggest and most influential **absolute** monarchy today is...
Iraq
Iran
Afghanistan
Pakistan
India
Egypt
United Arab Emirates
Saudi Arabia
Oman
Sudan
Yemen
Modern Saudi Arabia got its start in 1902 when **Abd al-Aziz ibn Saud** conquered Riyadh with an army of his brothers, cousins, and in-laws.
By 1925, Abd al-Aziz had defeated his main rivals in the region.
PRESENTING KING ABD AL-AZIZ IBN SAUD, SULTAN OF NAJD AND ITS DEPENDENCIES, KING OF THE HIJAZ!
THAT'S NOT GOING TO FIT ON A BUSINESS CARD. WHY DON'T WE JUST CALL IT ALL... SAUDI ARABIA?
Abd al-Aziz convened a council of influential citizens to help design the new government.
The **Shura Council** were merchants, former rulers Abd al-Aziz had defeated, and the ulama (powerful religious authorities who interpreted religious law and chose new rulers).

WE HAVE AGREED ON A "CONSULTATIVE ISLAMIC STATE."
FINE. BUT NO ELECTIONS.
AND THE KING MAKES THE LAWS.
THE ULAMA STILL *INTERPRET* THE LAWS, RIGHT?

AS LONG AS YOUR INTERPRETATION IS THAT *I* AM IN CHARGE.

Not everybody was on board with the new monarchy.

Over time, the royal family got less and less interested in consulting anyone else.
HE'S JUST NOT THAT INTO US ANYMORE.

Periodically, citizens would ask for a document that would lay down the basic rules of government, and the king would make promises.
1932: KING ABD AL-AZIZ AL-SAUD
OUR EXISTING COUNCIL OF DEPUTIES MUST IMMEDIATELY START THE DRAFTING OF A BASIC LAW OF GOVERNANCE FOR THE KINGDOM,
A LAW OF SUCCESSION TO THE THRONE, AND A LAW FOR GOVERNMENTAL ORGANIZATION.
Royal Order No. 2716
1962: CROWN PRINCE FAISAL
THE GOVERNMENT IS OF THE OPINION THAT THE TIME HAS NOW COME FOR THE PROMULGATION OF A FUNDAMENTAL LAW FOR THE COUNTRY...
1964: KING FAISAL APPOINTS A COMMITTEE TO DRAFT THE FUNDAMENTAL LAW.
1975: KING KHALID CROWNED, PROMISES A DRAFT LAW AND A CONSULTATIVE COUNCIL.
1980: CROWN PRINCE FAHD SAYS A 209-ARTICLE DRAFT IS READY TO BE SHARED.
1982: AT HIS CORONATION, KING FAHD PROMISES THE LAW WILL BE ANNOUNCED ANYTIME.
Nothing ever came of the promises. After all, things were pretty good from where the royal family sat.
ABDULLAH (CROWN PRINCE, FIRST DEPUTY PRIME MINISTER, KING'S BROTHER)
SULTAN (MINISTER OF DEFENSE AND AVIATION, SECOND DEPUTY PRIME MINISTER, KING'S BROTHER)
NAYEF (MINISTER OF INTERIOR, KING'S BROTHER)
FAHD (KING AND PRIME MINISTER)
SAUD AL-FAISAL (MINISTER OF FOREIGN AFFAIRS, KING'S NEPHEW)
THE DEMOCRATIC SYSTEM PREVAILING IN THE WORLD DOES NOT SUIT US IN THE REGION...

Things started to change in the early 1990s.
There was external pressure:

There were also internal demands for reform.

In December 1990, forty-three businessmen, technocrats, journalists, and liberal reformers published a petition calling for reform:

CREATE A CONSULTATIVE COUNCIL

EQUALITY UNDER THE LAW

ADDRESS CORRUPTION IN THE PROVINCIAL GOVERNMENTS

REFORM THE JUDICIAL SYSTEM

WOMEN'S RIGHTS

RESTRICT THE COMMITTEE FOR THE PROMOTION OF VIRTUE AND THE PREVENTION OF VICE

PRESS FREEDOM CONSISTENT WITH ISLAM

But in February 1991, almost two hundred of the most influential ulama, including the senior religious authority in Saudi Arabia, submitted their own petition.

CONFIRM SHARIA AS THE GUIDING LAW

COMBAT CORRUPTION

REFORM EMBASSIES

CHANGE FOREIGN POLICY TO FOLLOW MUSLIM VALUES

DISTRIBUTE WEALTH MORE EQUALLY

EMPOWER THE ARMY, RELIGIOUS INSTITUTIONS, AND THE JUDICIARY

Factions formed.

SO WHAT HAPPENED?
DID THE REFORMERS WIN?
King Fahd eventually agreed to some of the demands.
"THESE LAWS HAVE BEEN DRAWN UP AFTER A METICULOUS AND PATIENT STUDY...
CARRIED OUT BY A SELECT GROUP OF LEARNED MEN OF SOUND KNOWLEDGE AND EXPERIENCE...
"WE ARE CONFIDENT THAT THESE LAWS WILL, WITH THE HELP OF GOD...
ASSIST THE STATE IN REALIZING EVERY SAUDI CITIZEN'S HOPES FOR THE WELFARE AND PROGRESS OF THIS HOMELAND AND HIS ARAB AND ISLAMIC NATION."
But the Basic Law of 1992 ultimately didn't change much.
Article 5:
a. The system of government in Saudi Arabia shall be monarchical.
b. The dynasty right shall be confined to the sons of the Founder, King Abdul Aziz bin Abdul Rahman Al Saud (Ibn Saud), and the sons of sons...
WHO WROTE THIS THING?
THAT WOULD BE ME AND MY FAMILY.
WE DON'T EVEN GET A SAY IN PICKING THE NEW KING ANYMORE!
I HAVE SOME ADDITIONAL COMPLAINTS.

BUT HEY, YOU GOT YOUR CONSULTATIVE COUNCIL! THAT'S GOOD, RIGHT?
WE ASKED FOR MORE PEOPLE TO HAVE A ROLE IN DECISION-MAKING.
WHILE IT'S TRUE THAT THE MEMBERS OF THE CONSULTATIVE COUNCIL COME FROM RELIGIOUS, BUSINESS, AND ACADEMIC BACKGROUNDS...
SEE WHO CHOOSES THE MEMBERS OF THE COUNCIL?

THE KING! OH. HE CAN FIRE THEM, TOO, WHENEVER HE WANTS.
NOT TO MENTION THAT WOMEN WEREN'T INCLUDED UNTIL 2013.

IT'S THE SAME THING WITH JUDGES.
THE KING APPOINTS THEM ALL.

IN FACT, SEE ARTICLE 44?
ALL EXECUTIVE, LEGISLATIVE, AND JUDICIAL AUTHORITY ULTIMATELY BELONGS TO THE KING.
SO ALL THE CONSULTATIVE COUNCIL CAN REALLY DO IS MAKE RECOMMENDATIONS.
THE KING CAN IGNORE THEM.

ALL THESE NEW RULES AND INSTITUTIONS BOIL DOWN TO "THE KING STILL DOES WHAT HE WANTS"?
WE RESPECT TRADITION AND THE ROYAL FAMILY. WE JUST WANT A LITTLE MORE SAY IN DECISIONS.
AND IN OUR DAILY LIVES.
Almost all the power and wealth still belongs to the royal family, including how laws and policies are made.
Who sits at the table matters. If you control who sits at the table, you have a lot of power.
The Basic Law gave the Saudi people no way to hold their rulers accountable or make them change.
WHY WOULD PEOPLE TODAY LET A SINGLE PERSON HAVE THAT MUCH POWER?
It's very hard to change anything in an absolute monarchy unless the monarch wants it to change.
BUT WAIT, THIS BASIC LAW SOUNDS A LOT LIKE A CONSTITUTION.
WHY ISN'T SAUDI ARABIA A CONSTITUTIONAL MONARCHY?

In a **constitutional** monarchy, the monarch is still the head of state, but their power is limited. The country is governed by laws made by elected representatives.
The monarch is just one node in the network of institutions that make up the government.
GOVERNMENT DIRECTORY
MONARCH
PRIME MINISTER
JUDICIARY
PARLIAMENT
CITIZENS
SO, WHAT DOES THE MONARCH ACTUALLY DO, THEN?

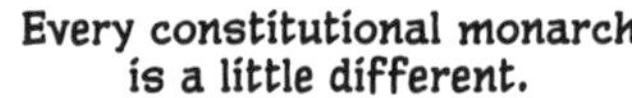

Every constitutional monarch is a little different.

Some monarchs call the legislature into session, approve laws before they go into effect, or appoint people to certain high offices. They might even be the head of the armed forces.

Many constitutional monarchs have a mostly ceremonial role.

WHY KEEP THE MONARCH AROUND AT ALL?

A lot of people ask that question.

THINK HOW MANY PEOPLE WE COULD HOUSE, FEED, AND EDUCATE WITH THAT MONEY!
BUT THE ROYALS ARE LIVING SYMBOLS OF OUR NATION!
YOU CAN'T MEASURE THEIR VALUE BY THE BUDGET!
HOW CAN A PERSON BE A SYMBOL OF A WHOLE NATION?
GOOD QUESTION. CAN ONE PERSON REALLY REPRESENT EVERYTHING A COUNTRY IS OR DOES?
Countries adopt symbols to stand in for the ideals their people aspire to uphold.
As a living symbol, monarchs can help people remain committed to those principles, even in challenging times.
Look at what King Haakon VII meant to the Norwegians in World War II.
YOUR MAJESTY, THE NAZIS SAY THEY'LL STOP INVADING...
IF YOU FIRE THE GOVERNMENT AND PUT VIDKUN QUISLING IN CHARGE.
NORWAY. APRIL 1940.

YOU TELL THEM I'LL ABDICATE THE THRONE BEFORE I GIVE THAT TRAITOR QUISLING CONTROL OVER NORWAY.

WAIT, IS ***THAT*** WHERE THE WORD ***QUISLING*** COMES FROM?

Norway regained its independence from Sweden in 1905. The Norwegians wrote a constitution and elected Haakon VII to be the first king of modern independent Norway.

But thirty-five years later, it looked like that story was about to end.

THEY SAY IF YOU REFUSE, THEY WILL DEPOSE YOU.

DO THEY THINK THREATS WILL CHANGE MY ANSWER?

JUNE 7, 1940. TROMSØ.
THE BRITISH NAVY HAVE A SHIP JUST OVER THAT HILL!
ONLY A LITTLE FARTHER, YOUR MAJESTY!

SOON AFTER...

I JUST HEARD ON THE RADIO:

THE ROYAL FAMILY HAS FLED TO ENGLAND!

YOU MEAN THEY'VE ABANDONED US? SOME KING!

RAGNHILDE

Haakon could have accepted exile in Great Britain. Instead, he and the royal family worked tirelessly to support the Norwegian resistance.

He refused over and over again to abdicate. Regular Norwegians rallied around him, even adopting his royal emblem as their symbol.
WE ARE HERE TO SUPPORT A FREE AND INDEPENDENT NORWAY!

HOW COULD THEY RALLY AROUND A KING WHO WASN'T EVEN IN THE COUNTRY?
THE NAZIS CRIMINALIZED SUPPORT FOR THE ROYAL FAMILY, SO WE GOT CREATIVE.
ARNE SKOUEN, NORWEGIAN JOURNALIST
FOR INSTANCE, THIS WAS 1941'S MOST POPULAR CHRISTMAS CARD.
THE LEFT SIDE SAYS "DOWN WITH THE NAZI PARTY, LONG LIVE THE KING."
NED MED N.S LEVE KONGEN
SALTEDE ISTER OLSON RPOSTEJ SGATE 40

Even kids were in on it.
HOW NICE TO HEAR CHILDREN SINGING!
HOLD ON A MINUTE...
UP WITH HAAKON, DOWN WITH QUISLING, HAAKON AND NO OTHER. HAAKON IS A FRIENDLY GUY, BUT QUISLING IS A BOTHER. I LIKE THE KING, AND THE KING, HE LIKES ME, FOR WE ARE NORWEGIANS, BOTH THE KING AND ME.

I'M STARTING TO SEE: PEOPLE REALLY FELT THE KING WAS STILL WITH THEM.

WHICH MEANT THE NORWAY THEY LOVED WAS STILL THERE, TOO.

I GUESS HE DIDN'T ABANDON US AFTER ALL.

HE MIGHT BE GONE, BUT WE AREN'T FORGOTTEN.

HANG ON A SECOND.

NORWAY IS A CONSTITUTIONAL MONARCHY. HAAKON WAS THE KING, BUT HE WASN'T REALLY IN CHARGE.

WHAT WAS THE ACTUAL GOVERNMENT DOING THIS WHOLE TIME?

The royal family and the elected government were in exile, and they all worked to support the resistance.
But without King Haakon, the elected government and the fighters on the ground would have drifted apart.
AND NOW, A CHRISTMAS MESSAGE FROM KING HAAKON VII TO THE PEOPLE OF NORWAY.

HEAVY CLOUDS HANG OVER US, BUT I URGE YOU TO CELEBRATE WITH CONFIDENCE AND FAITH IN THE FUTURE.
JUST AS I HAVE CONFIDENCE IN THE GOVERNMENT OF MR. NYGAARDSVOLD TO LEAD US THROUGH THIS DARK TIME...

YOU KNOW, I NEVER LIKED NYGAARDSVOLD.
HE DIDN'T KNOW WHAT WE NEEDED EVEN WHEN HE WAS IN THE COUNTRY.

BUT THE KING SAYS HE'S WORKING HARD FOR OUR CAUSE.
I GUESS IF THE KING SAYS SO, I'LL TRUST HIM.
King Haakon helped maintain the legitimacy of the government, even though the Nazis were working hard to sow distrust.

I WOULD NEVER HAVE BELIEVED PEOPLE WOULD TRUST A KING SO MUCH. ESPECIALLY A KING IN EXILE.

THEY COULDN'T SEE HIM. HE COULDN'T SAVE THEM FROM BEING KILLED.

BUT HE GAVE US HOPE THAT WE WOULD SURVIVE AND WIN OUR COUNTRY BACK.
THE KING HAD FAITH IN HIS PEOPLE, WHICH HELPED THEM STAY STRONG.
Even when they don't make the laws or have power over life and death, monarchs can be leaders their people respect and need.
Their leadership isn't limited to intangibles like hope. What King Bhumibol and Queen Sirikit gave the people of Thailand was extremely tangible.
"WE SHALL REIGN WITH RIGHTEOUSNESS..."
Bhumibol was crowned in 1950, during a period of political upheaval. The king's power was limited by the constitution and the ongoing threat of a military coup.
"...FOR THE BENEFITS AND HAPPINESS OF THE SIAMESE PEOPLE..."
THINK HE MEANS IT?
HE SOUNDS SINCERE...
I'LL BELIEVE IT WHEN I SEE SOME RESULTS.

King Bhumibol and Queen Sirikit traveled to the poorest and least developed areas of Thailand, learning directly from their people what they needed.
I SEE WHAT YOU MEAN. ALL THE SILT IS RUNNING RIGHT INTO THE RICE PADDY.
HOW MANY LANDSLIDES HAVE YOU HAD? WE HAVE TO DO SOMETHING ABOUT THIS.
WHY ISN'T THE ELECTED GOVERNMENT HELPING YOU?
HONEY, NO FANCY GOVERNMENT PERSON WOULD EVER COME OUT HERE.
HELPING US DOESN'T MAKE THEM RICH OR POWERFUL.
BUT THE KING AND QUEEN DON'T MIND GETTING A LITTLE DIRTY WITH US.
The king and queen funded thousands of Royal Development Projects to improve health, sanitation, transportation, agriculture, education, and infrastructure.
THIS IS VETIVER GRASS.
OUR EXPERTS SAY IT HELPS STOP EROSION AND STABILIZES THE GROUND.
IF WE PLANT IT, THE SOIL WILL STOP RUNNING DOWN INTO OUR RICE PADDIES?
AND THE HILL WILL STOP COLLAPSING ON OUR HOUSES?
THAT'S RIGHT. AND IT WILL GROW FAST IF YOU PLANT IT CORRECTLY.
SEE? WE HAD A PROBLEM, AND THE KING FIXED IT.

SERBIA
ETHIOPIA
NEPAL
MONACO
SPAIN
BELGIUM
RWANDA
GHANA
JORDAN
LUXEMBOURG
AFGHANISTAN
HUNGARY
NETHERLANDS
MOROCCO
ALBANIA
TUNISIA
LIECHTENSTEIN
MALAYSIA
LESOTHO
BULGARIA
KOREA
CAMBODIA
UNITED KINGDOM
HAITI
ALL RIGHT, MAYBE THERE'S A REASON SOME COUNTRIES HAVE HUNG ON TO THEIR ***KINGS AND QUEENS***.
BUT A LOT OF COUNTRIES ***HAVEN'T.*** THERE HAS TO BE A REASON FOR THAT, RIGHT?
AND IN A LOT OF COUNTRIES, THE MONARCH HAS GONE FROM THE BIG BOSS TO THIS LIVING SYMBOL THING.
WHY IS THAT?
Our expectations of monarchies have changed over time.
Originally, a monarch was the strongest person around, someone who was capable of protecting the people inside the territory they controlled from other strong people.
MINE
MINE
MINE
MINE
MINE
MINE
MINE
Eventually, monarchs started believing that they personally owned all the land, people, and things inside their territory.
It was all just property that came with being king or queen.

Many religions taught that monarchs were chosen by their gods to rule over other people.

As long as the monarch was upholding their responsibilities under divine law, there was no legitimate reason to deny their authority.

I REMEMBER THAT LINE FROM SAUDI ARABIA.

Kings called themselves the fathers of their nations. Denying the authority of the king was equated with denying the authority of parents over children, denying divine authority, and denying the basic social order.

THOSE ARE HIGH STAKES.
BUT CLAIMING DIVINE RIGHT OR CALLING YOURSELF "FATHER OF THE NATION" DOESN'T MAKE YOU A GOOD LEADER OR MEAN YOU HAVE GOOD IDEAS.
OTHER PEOPLE MIGHT HAVE GOOD IDEAS, TOO. EVEN IF THEY DON'T HAVE CROWNS.

Exactly.

As time passed, people around the world started thinking that more people should be involved in making decisions that affect our daily lives.

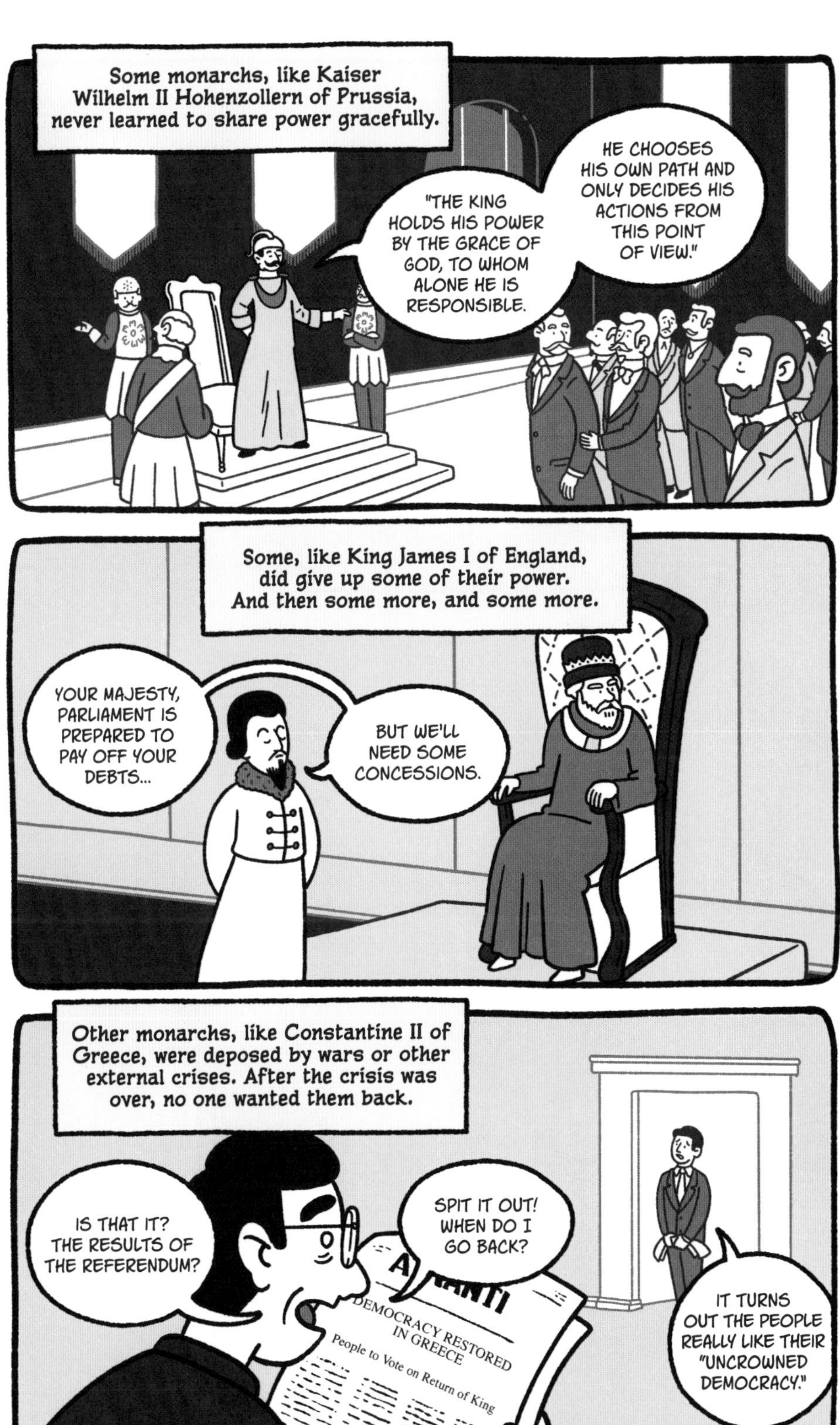
Some monarchs, like Kaiser Wilhelm II Hohenzollern of Prussia, never learned to share power gracefully.
"THE KING HOLDS HIS POWER BY THE GRACE OF GOD, TO WHOM ALONE HE IS RESPONSIBLE.
HE CHOOSES HIS OWN PATH AND ONLY DECIDES HIS ACTIONS FROM THIS POINT OF VIEW."
Some, like King James I of England, did give up some of their power. And then some more, and some more.
YOUR MAJESTY, PARLIAMENT IS PREPARED TO PAY OFF YOUR DEBTS...
BUT WE'LL NEED SOME CONCESSIONS.
Other monarchs, like Constantine II of Greece, were deposed by wars or other external crises. After the crisis was over, no one wanted them back.
IS THAT IT? THE RESULTS OF THE REFERENDUM?
SPIT IT OUT! WHEN DO I GO BACK?
DEMOCRACY RESTORED IN GREECE
People to Vote on Return of King
IT TURNS OUT THE PEOPLE REALLY LIKE THEIR "UNCROWNED DEMOCRACY."

Monarchs told their people they were in charge because they were special in some way.
They held onto their power by staying at the tippy top of the political pyramid.
Eventually, the people at the bottom realized how easy it is to knock the monarch off their perch.
GATE M46
FINAL BOARDING CALL
MONARCH AIR FLIGHT 2814
MONARCH AIR
MONARCH
GROUP 1

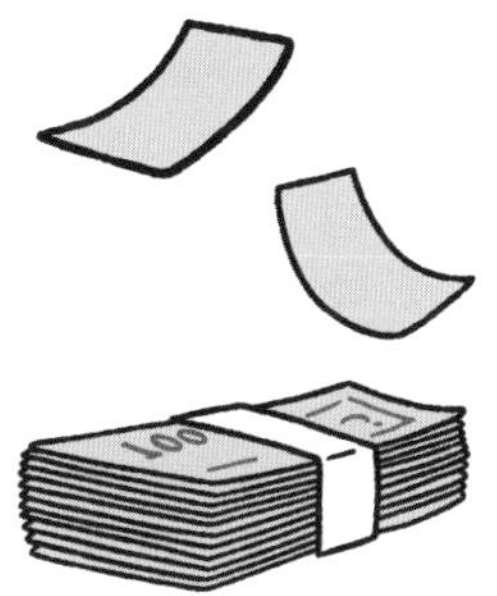

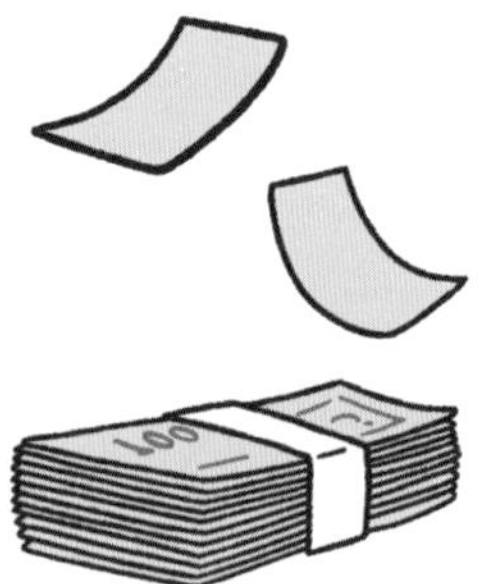

Dictators call themselves (and get called) many names.

WILL THE FOLLOWING PLEASE CHECK IN AT GATE 68:

DEAR LEADER KIM JONG-IL OF NORTH KOREA

SUPREME LEADER GETÚLIO VARGAS OF BRAZIL

FATHER OF NATIONS JOSEPH STALIN OF THE USSR

PRESIDENT FOR LIFE MOUSSA TRAORÉ OF MALI

AND *FATHER OF DEVELOPMENT* SUHARTO OF INDONESIA.

BUNCH OF *TYRANTS* AND *STRONGMEN!*

AUTOCRATS, ALL OF 'EM!

The terms can be confusing, but ultimately, they mean the same thing: *one* person holds *all* the power.

THAT'S THE SAME AS MONARCHS.
ALL THE POWER TO DECIDE ON LAW AND POLICY, CONTROL MONEY AND OTHER STATE RESOURCES...
THEY TELL CITIZENS HOW TO BEHAVE AND PUNISH PEOPLE WHO VIOLATE THEIR RULES?
OPEN
PAPER
That sums it up.

Some dictatorships have a military officer at the top. Some have a civilian. Sometimes dictators have so much power they resemble absolute monarchs.
WHAT'S THE DIFFERENCE BETWEEN A REALLY POWERFUL MONARCH AND A REALLY POWERFUL DICTATOR?
One difference is how they come to power.

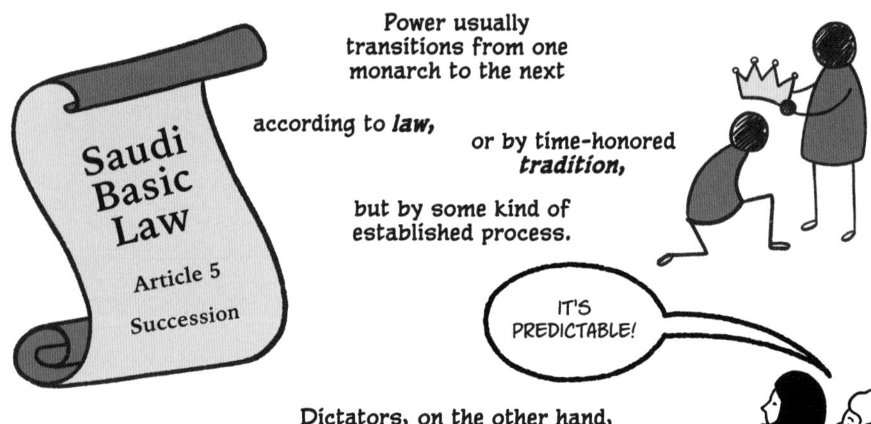

Power usually transitions from one monarch to the next
Saudi Basic Law
Article 5
Succession
according to *law,*
or by time-honored *tradition,*
but by some kind of established process.
IT'S PREDICTABLE!

Dictators, on the other hand, often come to power because of a ***breakdown*** in the normal process, sometimes even engineering these breakdowns to help their ambitions.

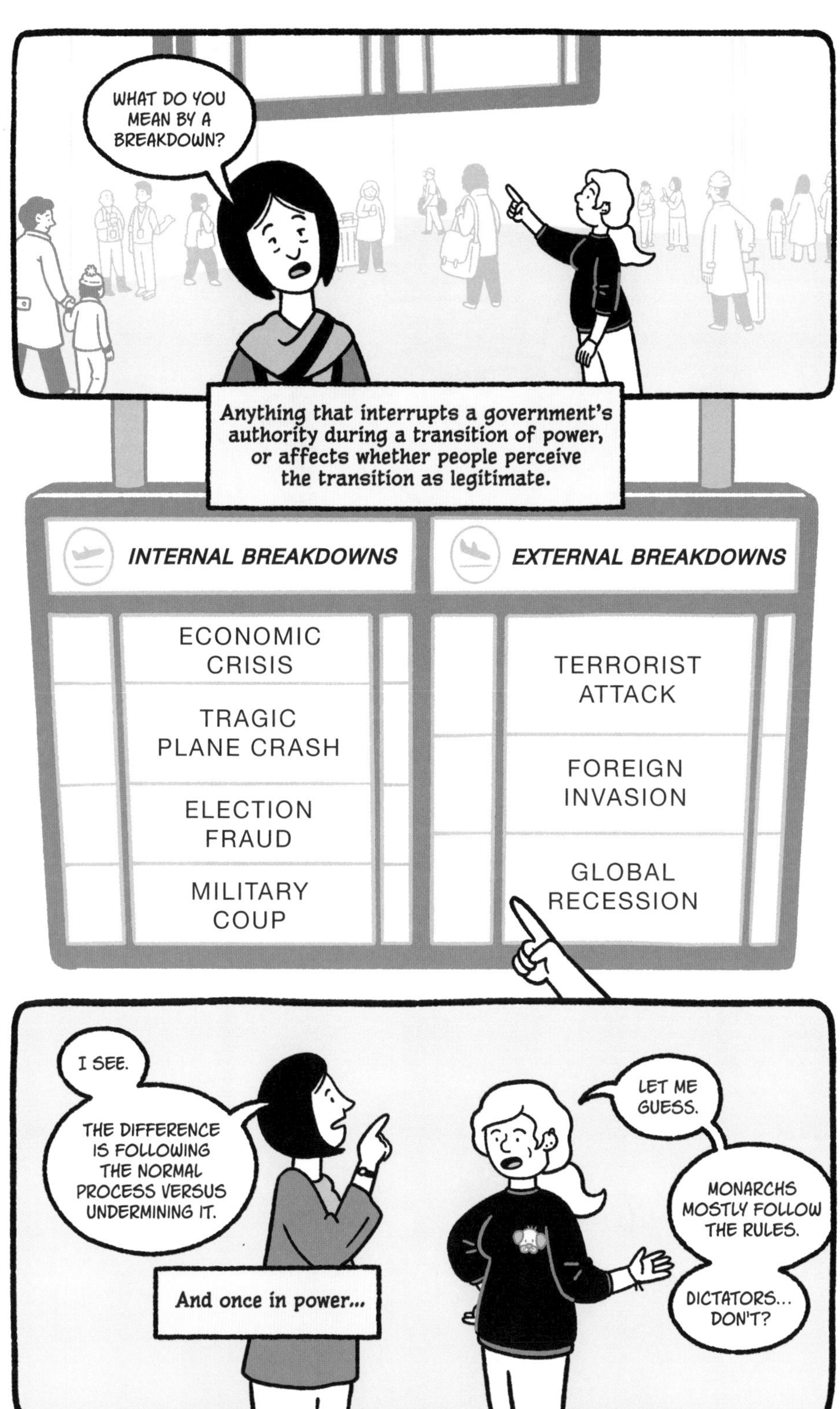
WHAT DO YOU MEAN BY A BREAKDOWN?
Anything that interrupts a government's authority during a transition of power, or affects whether people perceive the transition as legitimate.
INTERNAL BREAKDOWNS
ECONOMIC CRISIS
TRAGIC PLANE CRASH
ELECTION FRAUD
MILITARY COUP
EXTERNAL BREAKDOWNS
TERRORIST ATTACK
FOREIGN INVASION
GLOBAL RECESSION
I SEE.
THE DIFFERENCE IS FOLLOWING THE NORMAL PROCESS VERSUS UNDERMINING IT.
And once in power...
LET ME GUESS.
MONARCHS MOSTLY FOLLOW THE RULES.
DICTATORS... DON'T?

Monarchies might not be transparent or fair, but they are usually predictable.

Dictatorships, on the other hand, refuse to abide by normal political processes.

WHAT DO YOU MEAN I CAN'T MAKE NEW LAWS ALL BY MYSELF?

I HAVE TO GET PERMISSION FROM YOU GUYS TO SPEND MONEY?

I DON'T GET TO PUNISH PEOPLE FOR CRITICIZING ME?

THIS GOVERNING THING WILL BE A LOT MORE FUN IF WE DO IT *MY* WAY.

Dictators have their own rules for the institutions of government.

CHANGE • UNDERMINE • EXPLOIT • CO-OPT • CORRUPT

BREAKING

WE LOVE OUR LEADER

They rely on military and intelligence forces to compel the outcomes they want.

To keep citizens in line, they try to control avenues of information, through censorship or by co-opting the media.

BUT DICTATORS DON'T JUST DO AWAY WITH THE GOVERNMENT COMPLETELY, DO THEY?

Government institutions like legislatures and courts give a dictatorship the veneer of legitimacy.

But they're little more than facades.

A functioning government is like a well-lit room. There are many light sources, and each is supposed to perform a particular task.

Dictators take control by systematically turning off or redirecting all of the light sources.

If they have to, they'll rip the wires right out of the wall, but often they only have to change their focus.

In the end the fixtures are still there, but they only illuminate what the dictator wants to see.
OW! THAT'S MY FOOT!
NO, THAT'S *MY* FOOT!
WHEW. I DO *NOT* WANT TO GO BACK IN THERE.
THAT'S WHAT IT'S LIKE LIVING IN A DICTATORSHIP?
Redirecting the lights is only the beginning.
This is Uganda in January 1971.
Major General Idi Amin had just taken power in a military coup while President Milton Obote was out of the country.

Obote was on his way to becoming a dictator himself. He'd already suspended the constitution and canceled elections.

WHY THE LONG FACE? THIS IS A GREAT DAY FOR UGANDA!
THIS AMIN... HASN'T HE BEEN PART OF THE PROBLEM?
CORRUPTION, INTIMIDATING THE KING OF BUGANDA...
FAH! THAT'S ALL ON OBOTE'S HEAD.
ANYONE WOULD BE AN IMPROVEMENT, EVEN A CLOWN LIKE AMIN.
THE NEW LEADER HAS ORDERED ALL POLITICAL PRISONERS BE FREED.
FREE AND FAIR ELECTIONS WILL SOON BE HELD, GIVEN A STABLE SECURITY SITUATION...
THAT SOUNDS GOOD, BUT... I DON'T KNOW.
WE SHOULD GIVE HIM A CHANCE.
LISTEN! HE SAYS WE'LL HAVE ELECTIONS AGAIN SOON.
THINGS WILL BE CHANGED IN UGANDA.
WE WILL END ECONOMIC POLICIES THAT BENEFIT BIG, RICH MEN WHILE OTHER UGANDANS SUFFER...
FINALLY, SOMEONE WHO CARES ABOUT THE LITTLE PEOPLE!
IF THE ARMY GOES BACK TO THE BARRACKS, THIS COULD BE A GOOD CHANGE.

But the good feeling didn't last.
DID YOU HEAR ALL THAT SHOOTING OUT BY THE BARRACKS?
NO, BUT I HEARD SHOTS IN THE ARMY POST NEAR MY APARTMENT.
The people of Uganda became a captive audience as Amin turned the country into a one-man show.

He filled the government and the army with people who were personally loyal to him.

I HEARD FROM MY BROTHER...
...AMIN'S SOLDIERS WERE KILLING OBOTE'S PEOPLE.

THE ARMY WAS FIGHTING ITSELF?
NO, AMIN'S MEN MURDERED ACHOLI AND LANGI PEOPLE.
MY BROTHER SAW HUNDREDS OF BODIES.
HOW LONG BEFORE THE KILLING STOPS AND WE CAN GO BACK TO NORMAL?

By early 1972, around six thousand soldiers had been killed. Amin was already reneging on his early promises.
UPON FURTHER REFLECTION, I DO NOT BELIEVE THE SECURITY SITUATION WILL PERMIT ELECTIONS FOR AT LEAST FIVE YEARS.
I AM THE HERO OF AFRICA.
I CONSIDER MYSELF THE MOST POWERFUL FIGURE IN THE WORLD, AND THAT IS WHY I DO NOT LET ANY SUPERPOWER CONTROL ME.
He needed to be the center of everything, whether it was a photo or a country.
He even gave himself grandiose titles.
His Excellency, President for Life, Field Marshal Al Hadji Doctor Idi Amin Dada, VC, DSO, MC, Lord of All the Beasts of the Earth and Fishes of the Seas and Conqueror of the British Empire in Africa in General and Uganda in Particular
Amin thought of himself as the savior of Uganda, but he knew almost nothing about governing a country.

When Amin took power, Uganda had a thriving economy.
But he turned the government treasury into his personal bank account. When the money started running out, he ordered more printed.
WE CAN PRINT YOUR SHILLINGS AT ONCE, YOUR EXCELLENCY...
AS SOON AS WE RESOLVE THE MATTER OF HOW YOU WILL PAY US.
CONTRACT
PRINT THREE MILLION AND TAKE ONE MILLION FOR YOURSELF! JUST GET ME MY MONEY!
His troops followed his example, taking what they wanted.
I'M GOING TO NEED TO CONFISCATE YOUR WATCH.
AND YOUR WALLET.
AND YOUR CAR.
FOR NATIONAL SECURITY REASONS.
WE MIGHT NEED TO CONFISCATE YOUR SISTER, TOO.
UAZ 3252
But, after a year or two, even that wasn't enough.
FIELD MARSHAL, I HAVE TO TELL YOU THE TROOPS ARE GETTING RESTLESS.
THEIR MONEY DOESN'T GO VERY FAR THESE DAYS.
THERE'S PLENTY OF MONEY IN THIS COUNTRY. WE JUST HAVE TO GET IT INTO THE RIGHT HANDS.

WHERE'S MUSA?
AND NOW, A STATEMENT FROM HIS EXCELLENCY, PRESIDENT FOR LIFE, FIELD MARSHAL AL HADJI DOCTOR IDI AMIN DADA...
I HAVEN'T SEEN HIM SINCE HE WENT TO BRING HIS SISTER BACK TO KAMPALA FOR SCHOOL.

FELLOW CITIZENS, AS YOU KNOW, DREAMS COME TO ME FROM TIME TO TIME. THESE DREAMS COME FROM GOD.
LAST NIGHT I HAD SUCH A DREAM. GOD TOLD ME IT IS TIME TO FREE UGANDA FROM PARASITES WHO WANT TO TAKE EVERYTHING IN THIS COUNTRY FOR THEMSELVES.

IS HE TALKING ABOUT HIMSELF?
I REFER, OF COURSE, TO THESE ASIAN IMPERIALISTS WHO ARE HOARDING OUR WEALTH!

WHAT DOES HE MEAN?
MY FAMILY HAS LIVED HERE FOR THREE GENERATIONS!

There were more than fifty thousand people of South Asian descent living in Uganda.

They were the backbone of the middle class: doctors, lawyers, accountants, engineers, mechanics, and small business owners.

Amin gave them a choice: leave the country within ninety days, or be put in a detention camp.

THAT'S NOT A "CHOICE."

WE CAN'T PACK UP A LIFE AND A BUSINESS JUST LIKE THAT!

WHERE WILL WE GO?

But Amin didn't intend for them to pack anything. In fact, he forbade it. Each person was permitted to take $100 with them, but nothing else.

PHOTOS

WHAT ABOUT PROPERTY RIGHTS? WHY DIDN'T THEY GO TO THE COURTS?
IF PEOPLE WERE GETTING SHOT AND KICKED OUT OF THE COUNTRY, I WOULDN'T WANT TO BE THE JUDGE TELLING IDI AMIN NO.
YOU'RE RIGHT. I KEEP THINKING THERE HAD TO BE SOMEONE WHO COULD STOP HIM.
BUT I GUESS HE HAD ALL THE MONEY AND ALL THE GUNS.
Asian-owned business were the engine of the economy, but the new owners didn't know what they were doing.
CLOSED
Exports plummeted.
FOR RENT
Work dried up.
CLOSED
Even basic goods were hard to find.

I WENT FOR GROCERIES. THE SHELVES WERE EMPTY. I COULDN'T EVEN FIND SALT.
HOW DO I TEACH IF MY STUDENTS DON'T HAVE PENCILS AND PAPER?
WE'VE GIVEN UP ON OUR TEA AND COTTON.
WE'RE DOING ALL WE CAN JUST TO GROW ENOUGH TO EAT.

HAS ANYONE FOUND SOMEWHERE YOU CAN STILL BUY SOAP?
WHO COULD AFFORD IT?
YOU WORK IN A PRIVATE CLINIC, THOUGH. AREN'T THE SALARIES GOOD THERE?

DIDN'T YOU HEAR?
WHAT?
NO!
WHAT HAPPENED?

ONE OF AMIN'S GIRLFRIENDS GOT AN ABORTION IN A PRIVATE CLINIC LAST MONTH.
AMIN CLOSED ALL THE PRIVATE CLINICS IN REVENGE.

WHAT IS THIS COUNTRY COMING TO?
SHHH! YOU KNOW WHAT HAPPENS IF YOU SPEAK AGAINST AMIN.

More and more skilled, educated people fled Uganda.
Those who stayed suffered more every day.
Amin paid no attention to public services or national infrastructure.
Even if he had, many of the people who kept the lights on and the trains running had fled the country.
DID THIS GUY DO EVEN ONE GOOD THING?
I GUESS IT DEPENDS ON YOUR PERSPECTIVE.
LUNCH IS ON ME TODAY, BOYS!

YOU'D THINK PEOPLE WOULD GET FED UP AND START PROTESTING.
ZOOM

"We workers, peasants, and soldiers of Uganda want an end to killings, beatings, and kidnappings. We are tired of Amin, his lies, his murders, and his Government of scarcity. We want a country where our children can grow up as human beings. We are tired of fearing you, Amin. We want sugar, hoes, and soap. We want good transportation and not tanks and jets. The workers and peasants and even soldiers will put an end to Amin. People of Uganda rise up and stop this oppression."

Amin met any opposition, no matter how mild, with extreme brutality. His regime killed 300,000 people in eight years.
NOT TO MENTION THOSE HE TORTURED.
OR THE ONES WHO JUST... DISAPPEARED.

Some of his victims opposed what he was doing to Uganda.
ARCHBISHOP JANANI LUWUM

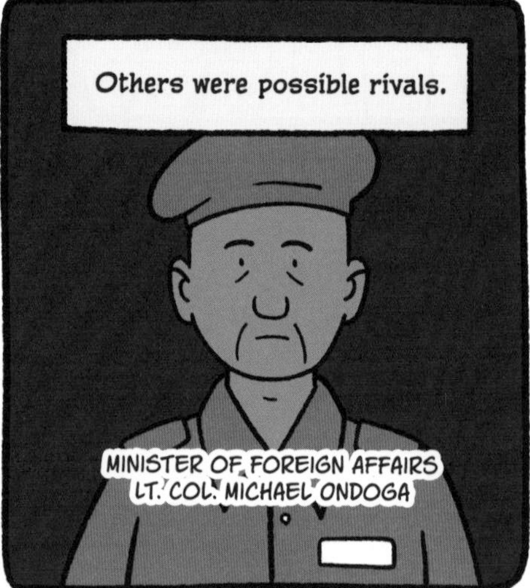
Others were possible rivals.
MINISTER OF FOREIGN AFFAIRS
LT. COL. MICHAEL ONDOGA

A few were killed to settle personal vendettas.
AMIN'S WIFE KAY ADROA

But most suffered simply because they had something Amin or his allies wanted.
RESOURCES
MONEY
LAND

THE POWER WAS OUT AT MULAGO HOSPITAL AGAIN LAST NIGHT.

EVERYWHERE ELSE IN KAMPALA, TOO.

THEY SAY...

SO MANY BODIES ARE THROWN IN THE RIVER THAT THEY INTERFERE WITH THE HYDROPOWER PLANT.

Idi Amin was eventually forced out of power in April 1979 by a coalition of Ugandan rebels and the Tanzanian army after he tried to invade Tanzania.
LIBERATION FORCES ENTERED KAMPALA TODAY, AFTER SIX MONTHS OF FIGHTING.
OUSTED DICTATOR IDI AMIN, REVILED ACROSS THE WORLD AS THE BUTCHER OF UGANDA, HAS REPORTEDLY FLED THE COUNTRY.
IS IT OVER? *REALLY* OVER?
I DON'T KNOW, BUT MAYBE WE CAN FINALLY GET OUR NORMAL LIVES BACK.
WELL, SOME OF US CAN.
When Amin took power, Uganda was known as the "Pearl of Africa."
It's not only what the dictator does while in power. It's about the mess a dictatorship leaves behind.

THAT WAS SO MUCH WORSE THAN MERELY TURNING OFF THE LIGHTS.

OKAY, THIS IS GOING TO SOUND WEIRD, BUT... I KIND OF FEEL BETTER NOW?
HOW COULD *THAT* MAKE YOU FEEL BETTER?

MY UNCLE IS ALWAYS SAYING AMERICA IS SECRETLY A DICTATORSHIP AND WE DON'T EVEN KNOW IT.
AND... MY UNCLE'S SMART. I WORRIED HE WAS RIGHT.

BUT YOU SAW. WHEN A DICTATOR SHOWS UP, HE DESTROYS EVERYTHING AND TAKES THE GOOD PARTS FOR HIM AND HIS FRIENDS.
YES, BUT—

SO YOU CAN'T EVER ACCIDENTALLY FALL INTO DICTATORSHIP.
IT'S NOT, LIKE, SUBTLE.
I'M NOT SURE IT'S ALWAYS THAT CLEAR...

Sometimes the lights go out quickly. Sometimes people don't realize they're living in the dark until it's too late.
Consider Lima, Peru, in 1990.
This is *Alberto Fujimori.*
I DON'T HAVE TO TELL YOU ABOUT THE ECONOMIC CRISIS. YOU'RE LIVING IT!
I'VE NEVER EVER SEEN ANYTHING LIKE THIS.
YOU'D NEVER BELIEVE HE'S JUST SOME PROFESSOR.
HAS HE EVER BEEN IN GOVERNMENT AT ALL?
SO IS GUZMÁN, AND LOOK WHAT HE'S DONE.
THOSE POLITICIANS FROM ARPA AND IZQUIERDA UNIDA DON'T CARE HOW YOU SUFFER.
THEY SIT COMFORTABLY ON THE OTHER SIDE OF THIS WALL OF SHAME.
WE ARE NOT SAFE! SENDERO LUMINOSO TERRORISTS ARE ATTACKING INNOCENT PEOPLE, DESTROYING HOMES, THREATENING OUR CHILDREN!

Sendero Luminoso, or the Shining Path, was a Maoist guerilla insurgency led by Abimael Guzmán.
In the 1980s, Sendero Luminoso fought a vicious war against the democratic government, which it funded through drug trafficking.
By the 1990 election, more than fifteen thousand people had died and Peru was the largest supplier of coca leaf in the world.
LIVE
THE GOVERNMENT HAS NEVER BEEN LESS POPULAR.
AND THIS "CHINO FUJIMORI" IS SAYING WHAT PEOPLE WANT TO HEAR.
BUT CAN HE DELIVER ON HIS OUTLANDISH PROMISES?
THERE'S JUST NO WAY TO KNOW!
Peru was also in the middle of an economic crisis. Jobs were scarce. Unemployment was high. Hyperinflation made basic goods extremely expensive.
Voters were looking for someone to blame.
WE KNOW THE SOURCE OF OUR TROUBLES!
WE HAVE JACKALS IN THE JUDICIARY! WE HAVE CORRUPTION AND INEFFICIENCY IN CONGRESS!
HE'S GOT A POINT.
WHEN WAS THE LAST TIME YOU HEARD OF A JUDGE WHO *WASN'T* TAKING BRIBES?

They were also looking for someone to fix the problems.
SOLUTIONS COME WHEN WE DO AWAY WITH POLITICAL PARTIES!
ELECT ME, AND I PROMISE YOU CHANGE!
CAMBIO!
CAMBIO!
CAMBIO 90 Y FUJIMORI!

I THINK HE MIGHT ACTUALLY WIN.
HE'S GOT THAT OUTSIDER ENERGY.
And he did.

At first, he seemed to be fixing Peru's problems, if not quite how he had promised.
INTERNATIONAL MONETARY FUND
PRIVATIZING STATE-OWNED ENTERPRISES, PAYING DOWN FOREIGN DEBT...
THIS FUJIMORI GUY IS A MIRACLE WORKER!
INTERNATIONAL MONETARY FUND:
Can Fujishock Save Peru?

BUT HE'S NOT EXACTLY PERFORMING MIRACLES AGAINST UNEMPLOYMENT OR CHOLERA.
AND WHY IS ALL THE MONEY GOING TO SOMETHING CALLED THE "MINISTRY OF THE PRESIDENCY"?
As much as his reforms helped Peru, they helped Fujimori more.

He replaced corrupt judges and other officials...with people loyal to him.

His economic reforms grew the national budget by twenty-five times during his first term...and that new revenue went to agencies he controlled.

He reorganized the military and intelligence services to fight Sendero Luminoso, coincidentally appointing his closest allies to senior posts.

THAT'S VLADIMIRO MONTESINOS, THE PRESIDENT'S CAMPAIGN LAWYER.

HE GOT KICKED OUT OF THE ARMY FOR SPYING BACK IN '76.

FORGET ALL THAT. LOOK AT MY RESULTS!

LIVE

GUZMÁN ARRESTED

Capturing the leader of Sendero Luminoso made Fujimori even more popular.

However, some people were starting to have concerns.

WE'VE GOTTEN CREDIBLE REPORTS OF MASS MURDER AND TORTURE IN THE NAME OF FIGHTING SENDERO LUMINOSO.

THEY SAY THE RECESSION IS OVER, BUT YOU'D NEVER KNOW IT FROM HERE.

Fujimori was good at making his critics seem like the real threat.

WE KNOW THAT THE TERRORISTS AND THEIR FRONT ORGANIZATIONS, OR USEFUL IDIOTS, WILL NOT GIVE UP...

THEY WILL USE ALL POSSIBLE RESOURCES TO HARM THE IMAGE OF PERU BY ALLEGING THAT OUR ARMED FORCES VIOLATE HUMAN RIGHTS.

I DON'T LIKE WHERE THIS IS GOING.

Eventually even some of his supporters thought things had gone too far.

They didn't understand how far Fujimori was willing to go.
"THE COUNTRY CANNOT CONTINUE TO BE WEAKENED BY TERRORISM, DRUG TRAFFICKING, AND CORRUPTION.
"THE POLITICAL CORRUPTION AND THE INFILTRATION HAVE REACHED SUCH A DEGREE THAT IT CAN BE FOUND IN ALL LEVELS AND RULINGS OF THE JUDICIAL POWER.
"THEREFORE, I AM SUSPENDING CERTAIN ARTICLES OF THE CONSTITUTION."
HANG ON. *WHAT?*

THIS IS THE END OF THE BRIBE-OCRACY. WE ARE BEGINNING A SEARCH FOR A MORE AUTHENTIC DEMOCRACY.
THERE ARE GOING TO BE SOME BIG CHANGES, JUST AS WE PROMISED.

NO ONE ASKED FOR THIS MUCH CHANGE!
WE WANTED HIM TO PAY OFF PERU'S DEBT, NOT REINVENT DEMOCRACY!
WHO DOES DEMOCRACY SERVE WHEN HALF THE POPULATION IS DYING OF HUNGER?

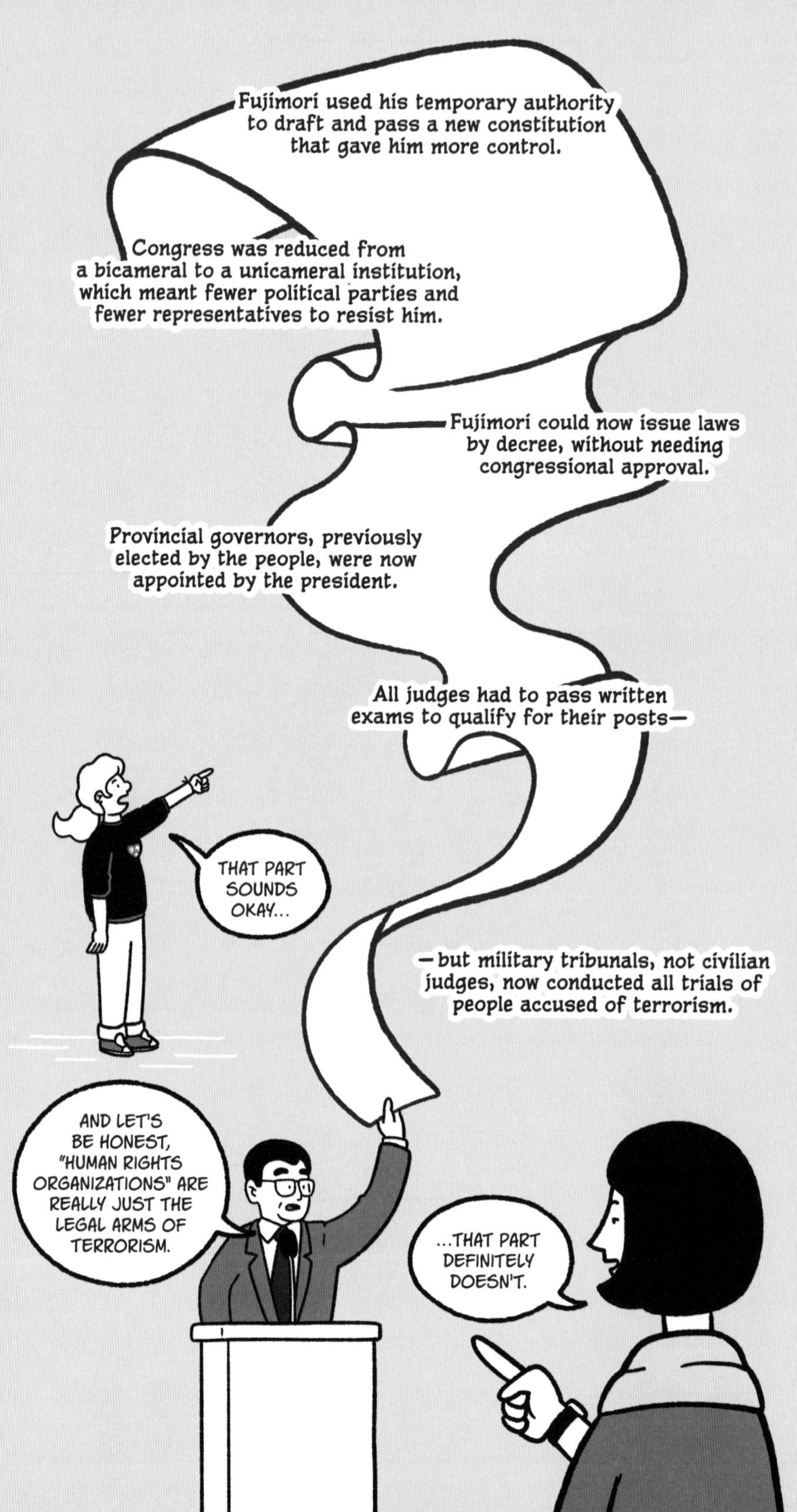

Fujimori used his temporary authority to draft and pass a new constitution that gave him more control.
Congress was reduced from a bicameral to a unicameral institution, which meant fewer political parties and fewer representatives to resist him.
Fujimori could now issue laws by decree, without needing congressional approval.
Provincial governors, previously elected by the people, were now appointed by the president.
All judges had to pass written exams to qualify for their posts—
THAT PART SOUNDS OKAY...
—but military tribunals, not civilian judges, now conducted all trials of people accused of terrorism.
AND LET'S BE HONEST, "HUMAN RIGHTS ORGANIZATIONS" ARE REALLY JUST THE LEGAL ARMS OF TERRORISM.
...THAT PART DEFINITELY DOESN'T.

The military also gained enormous new powers.
They could do house-to-house searches for suspected terrorists and occupy university campuses.
Senior generals were now appointed and removed by Fujimori, not the senate, so they owed their positions solely to him.
Military personnel were given amnesty for human rights abuses they committed as part of the war on terror.
COLINA GROUP = MURDERERS
LA CANTUTA 10 NO OLVIDA

DON'T TALK SO LOUD... IN FUJIMORI'S PERU, ***QUIEN HABLA ES TERRORISTA.***

DON'T PAY TOO MUCH ATTENTION TO THE DISCREDITED LEFT.

THEY'RE ALL TERRORIST SYMPATHIZERS ANYWAY.

Whenever people started complaining, Fujimori reminded them what was at stake.

DO YOU WANT THE RECESSION BACK? OR MAYBE YOU MISS THE DRUG TRAFFICKING?

SAY IT WITH ME: ***EL PERÚ NO PUEDE PARAR!***

MORE AND MORE CRIMES ARE TREATED AS TERRORISM THESE DAYS.
THEFT, ROBBERY, KIDNAPPING, ASSAULT...
MILITARY TRIBUNALS SHOULDN'T BE MORE POWERFUL THAN CIVILIAN COURTS.
SURELY PEOPLE DON'T REALLY BELIEVE THEY'RE CONSTANTLY SURROUNDED BY TERRORISTS?
PEOPLE BELIEVE IT BECAUSE THERE WAS VIOLENCE EVERYWHERE IN THE DAYS OF THE WAR.
BUS BOMBS, CAR BOMBS, MAIL BOMBS...
ABDUCTIONS, ASSASSINATIONS...
SOME OF IT WAS SENDERO LUMINOSO, SOME WAS THE PARAMILITARIES.
BUT WE ALL KNEW TO BE AFRAID.
FUJIMORI MAKES SURE HIS MESSAGE, AND ONLY HIS MESSAGE, IS SPREAD—
—BY BUYING, BLACKMAILING, AND THREATENING MEDIA ORGANIZATIONS.

WHAT HAPPENS IF THE MEDIA DOESN'T PLAY ALONG?

WHO IS THAT?

BARUCH IVCHER. HE USED TO OWN THE TV STATION FRECUENCIA LATINA.

THEY REPORTED ON ALL THE ABUSES OF THE REGIME.

TORTURE, MURDER...

MONTESINOS

THE WHOLE HORROR SHOW!

BREAKING NEWS

CORRUPTION IN GOVERNMENT

I JUST GOOGLED FUJIMORI, AND IT SAYS HE WON ***TWO MORE ELECTIONS*** EVEN AFTER HE DID ALL THAT STUFF.
WHY WOULD ANYONE VOTE FOR A DICTATOR?!

I DON'T LIKE EVERYTHING HE DOES...
BUT I ***REALLY*** DON'T WANT TO GO BACK TO THE BAD OLD DAYS OF THE INSURGENCY.

YOU CAN'T REALLY BLAME FUJIMORI.
HE'S HAD TO BE REAL TOUGH TO GET ALL THOSE CORRUPT JACKALS OUT OF OFFICE.

THANKS TO HIM, THINGS ARE FINALLY STABILIZING AFTER SO MANY HARD YEARS.

THE HARD TRUTH IS SOME PEOPLE ARE SUFFERING LESS THAN OTHERS.
INDIGENOUS PERUVIANS SUFFER HARSHER TREATMENT FROM FUJIMORI THAN THOSE DESCENDED FROM SPAIN.
AND IT'S OUR INDIGENOUS PEOPLES WHO TEND TO BE POOR, AND THE SPANISH-DESCENDED PERUVIANS WHO TEND TO BE WEALTHY.

Fujimori strategically deployed state resources to win elections.
NM
CAMBIO
NUEVA MAYORIA
CAMBIO
IT'S TIME FOR SOME SOCIAL IMPROVEMENT PROGRAMS.
LET'S BUILD SCHOOLS, REPAIR ROADS, END CHOLERA, AND MOST IMPORTANT, PUT PEOPLE BACK TO WORK!
SIR, WE DIDN'T EXACTLY GIVE THE MINISTRIES OF EDUCATION OR HEALTH ANY MONEY...

WHY GET THOSE BUREAUCRATS INVOLVED?
WE'LL PAY FOR IT ALL THROUGH THE MINISTRY OF THE PRESIDENCY.
AND YOU MAKE SURE EVERY BRICK AND PILL AND PAYCHECK HAS MY NAME ON IT.

AMBULAN
laRazón
FUJIMORI WINS REELECTI
IN LANDSLIDE
Defeats Javier Pérez de Cuéllar, former UN Secretary General

Between strategic public works projects and threat-focused propaganda, Fujimori remained popular for a long time.
The Maoist insurgency had been defeated, his political opponents were disorganized, and the military was still firmly behind him.

CAN I GET YOU ANYTHING ELSE, SIR?
LET ME THINK...

YES, I'LL TAKE A THIRD TERM.

TECHNICALLY THE CONSTITUTION DOESN'T ALLOW THAT, SIR.
LET'S ASK CONGRESS WHAT THEY THINK.

OH, NO PROBLEM, WE AGREE:
A MORE AUTHENTIC INTERPRETATION OF THE CONSTITUTION PERMITS YOU TO RUN AGAIN.
Of course, this agreement didn't happen without a few bribes and threats.

CAFE
I READ THAT HE FIRED ALL THREE OF THE CONSTITUTIONAL COURT JUDGES WHO TRIED TO ENFORCE TERM LIMITS.
CAN HE DO THAT?
I THOUGHT ALL THOSE PEOPLE WHO CALLED HIM A DICTATOR WERE BEING HYSTERICAL.
BUT THIS DOESN'T SEEM VERY DEMOCRATIC.
I HEAR THEY CALL HIM "CHINOCHET" ON THE STREET.
IF HE WOULD DO THIS, MAYBE THOSE RUMORS ABOUT DEATH SQUADS AREN'T JUST RUMORS...
Even with the propaganda, scare tactics, mass incarceration, and use of state resources to buy support, opposition kept growing.
I'M TIRED OF THE ARMY SEARCHING MY HOUSE IN CASE I'VE BEEN KEEPING A TERRORIST IN THE CUPBOARD FOR FIVE YEARS.
I'D LIKE TO KEEP SOME *FOOD* IN THE CUPBOARD...
BUT WE'RE STILL WAITING FOR THAT GREAT ECONOMY FUJIMORI PROMISED.
Fujimori's economic reforms ended hyperinflation, but never delivered higher salaries or lower unemployment.

Businesses and the media were tired of threats and extortion.
HERE'S TODAY'S NEWS...
PERSONALLY APPROVED BY THE PRESIDENT.
ACTUALLY, I'M DONE BEING TOLD WHAT TO BROADCAST ALL THE TIME.
YOU DON'T WANT US TO BRING OUT... THE TAPE, DO YOU?
YOU KNOW WHAT? MAYBE I'VE GOT SOME TAPES OF MY OWN.
BUT HE GOT REELECTED IN 2000! AGAIN!
ONLY BECAUSE HE CHEATED SO MUCH IN THE FIRST ROUND THAT THE OPPOSITION BOYCOTTED THE RUNOFF VOTE!
WHAT A SURPRISE.

Ultimately, Fujimori's tactics were his undoing.
VIDEO LEAKED TODAY SHOWS FUJIMORI'S RIGHT-HAND MAN VLADIMIRO MONTESINOS PERSONALLY HANDING A CONGRESSMAN A $15,000 BRIBE.
THIS SHOCKING DEVELOPMENT COMES ONLY WEEKS AFTER FUJIMORI WON REELECTION.
BREAKING NEWS
MONTESINOS FLEES TO PANAMA

PROTESTS ARE ERUPTING IN THE STREETS OF LIMA—
WAIT, THIS JUST IN:
MORE THAN 2,400 VIDEOS HAVE BEEN FOUND IN THE APARTMENT OF MONTESINOS, ALL OF WHICH SHOW "THE DOCTOR" COERCING GOVERNMENT AND MEDIA FIGURES.

Bribes to keep TV stations from showing interviews with the opposition.
Bribes to cancel investigations into paramilitary activity.
Bribes to judges to influence the outcome of cases.
BUT FUJIMORI GOT ELECTED IN THE FIRST PLACE BECAUSE HE WAS GOING TO FIGHT CORRUPTION!

It was the last straw.
In November 2000, after calling for new elections, Fujimori left Peru for Japan.
Congress stripped him of the presidency, and new elections were set for August 2001.

Fujimori attempted a comeback in 2005. But he was arrested and extradited back to Peru.

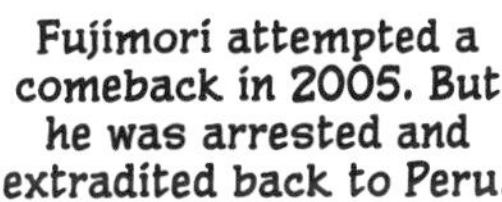

In 2009, Fujimori was sentenced to twenty-five years in prison for crimes against humanity, including the La Cantuta abductions and murders.

THAT WAS WHAT HE GAVE THE MILITARY AMNESTY FOR, RIGHT?
IT WAS HIS FORCES ALL ALONG, NOT SOME MYSTERIOUS "TERRORISTS." THE HYPOCRITE!

SO HE DIDN'T WIN AFTER ALL!
IT DEPENDS ON WHAT YOU MEAN.
HE WON REELECTION, THEN HE WAS OUSTED...
BUT NOT BEFORE ALL THOSE PEOPLE GOT TORTURED OR KILLED.

IT DOESN'T SOUND LIKE HE FIXED THE ECONOMIC PROBLEMS.

Fujimori left behind the ghost of a government with little authority or legitimacy.

Corruption is still one of the biggest problems in Peru.
WE WORKED SO HARD TO BUILD A DEMOCRACY.
AND HE TOOK IT APART SO THAT HE COULD DO THINGS HIS WAY.
IT DOESN'T REALLY FEEL LIKE A WIN ANYMORE.

IF THE CONSEQUENCES ARE ALWAYS SO BAD...
WHY AREN'T WE MORE VIGILANT AGAINST DICTATORS?
Times of crisis are tense and uncertain. Dictators often come to power because they seem like they can control what's going on.

WHEN YOU'RE SCARED IT'S NICE TO THINK THAT SOMEONE ELSE WILL FIX IT.
EVEN WHEN THEIR "SOLUTION" WILL CLEARLY MAKE EVERYTHING WORSE?
It's not always easy to tell.

Dictators are often charismatic populists promising to change a government people don't like.
I WILL NEVER PLAY POLITICS AS USUAL!
I'M AN OUTSIDER AND I HATE POLITICIANS AS MUCH AS YOU DO!
THIS GUY IS THE REAL DEAL!
THE FAT CAT POLITICIANS ARE AFRAID OF HIM!
YEAH, HE'S REALLY GONNA SHAKE UP THE SYSTEM!
Even the Founders, like Alexander Hamilton, worried about how appealing dictators could be.
HISTORY WILL TEACH US THAT OF THOSE MEN WHO HAVE OVERTURNED THE LIBERTIES OF REPUBLICS...
THE GREAT NUMBER HAVE BEGUN THEIR CAREER BY PAYING AN OBSEQUIOUS COURT TO THE PEOPLE;
COMMENCING DEMAGOGUES AND ENDING TYRANTS.
Institutions often aren't prepared for a direct assault, especially in democracies.
WE DON'T *WANT* TO BELIEVE THAT OUR LEADER DOESN'T CARE ABOUT US AT ALL.
OR THAT WE CHOSE SOMEONE WHO WOULD TWIST OUR GOVERNMENT FOR THEIR OWN BENEFIT.
WE TELL OURSELVES SOMEONE WILL STOP THEM BEFORE THEY GO TOO FAR.
WE WANT TO GIVE THEM THE BENEFIT OF THE DOUBT, EVEN WHEN WE SEE THEM TURNING OFF THE LIGHTS.

SO MY UNCLE WAS RIGHT.
A DICTATORSHIP REALLY CAN CREEP UP ON US.
There are always warning signs.
Steven Levitsky and Daniel Ziblatt, who study dictatorships in Europe and South America, tell us to watch out for would-be leaders who:
Reject the existing rules of politics with their words and actions
Tolerate, or even encourage, violence
Try to silence, undermine, or minimize dissent
and
Are willing to limit civil liberties.
HOLD ON, I'M TAKING NOTES.
MAYBE THIS IS A SILLY QUESTION, BUT IS THERE SUCH A THING AS A BENEVOLENT DICTATOR?
SOMEONE WHO HAS ALL THE POWER, BUT USES IT FOR GOOD?
I MEAN, IN THE PUBLIC INTEREST?
It's not impossible.

Someone could have all the power, understand how to use it to benefit the most people, and then choose to use it that way.
THAT SOUNDS KIND OF LIKE THOSE VIRTUOUS RULERS ALL THE PHILOSOPHERS TALKED ABOUT.
GOOD POINT.
A BENEVOLENT DICTATOR IS PROBABLY ABOUT AS LIKELY AS A PHILOSOPHER-KING.

I GUESS IT DOESN'T MATTER WHAT WE CALL THEM.
IF ONE PERSON HAS ALL THE POWER ***AND*** WEALTH, THEY'LL ALWAYS BE ABLE TO SHUT THE DOOR WHEN SOMEONE DISAGREES WITH THEM.
OR WORSE.
THERE'S SIMPLY NO WAY TO KEEP THEM FROM GOING DOWN A DANGEROUS PATH.

BY THE TIME YOU GET THINGS BACK UNDER CONTROL, A LOT OF DAMAGE HAS BEEN DONE.
TO THE ECONOMY. TO PUBLIC TRUST IN GOVERNMENT.
TO THE WAY THE LEGISLATURE, COURTS, AND ALL OTHER INSTITUTIONS WORK TOGETHER.
AND TO REAL PEOPLE.

EXIT TO MAIN CONCOURSE

LET'S TRY SOMETHING ELSE.

IS THIS WHERE WE FIND CONGRESS? THAT'S JUST A FEW PEOPLE, AND THEY HAVE A LOT OF POWER.

BUT THEY STILL HAVE TO WIN ELECTIONS AND WORK WITH THE OTHER BRANCHES OF GOVERNMENT.

In some societies, a small number of people have the power to make decisions and resolve disputes, accountable only to themselves.

BEEP

BEEP

This is different from governments where one person makes decisions.

BEEEP

THANKS BUT NO THANKS.

It's also different from governments where all adult citizens have a say.
BEEP
BEEP
MOVE OUTTA THE WAY!
ALL FAITH CHAPEL
WHY PUT EVERYONE IN CHARGE WHEN SOME OF US ARE BORN TO IT?
OR HAVE A DIRECT LINE TO THE DIVINE?
ARISTOCRATS & THEOCRATS
SNACKS
WHY BOTHER GOVERNING WHEN I CAN TAKE WHAT I WANT?
NOT IF I TAKE IT FIRST!
WARLORDS
VIP LOUN
WE'RE RICH ENOUGH TO GET WHAT WE WANT OUT OF POLITICS, NO MATTER WHO SITS IN THE BIG CHAIR.
OLIGARCHS
SOMETIMES IT MAKES SENSE TO PUT JUST A FEW PEOPLE IN CHARGE...

WE SAW WHAT HAPPENS WHEN ONLY ONE PERSON'S OPINION MATTERS.
MAYBE IT'S BETTER TO HAVE A SMALL TEAM WORKING TOGETHER?
IF WE'RE GOING TO HAND OVER POWER TO JUST A FEW PEOPLE, THEY REALLY NEED TO BE THE *RIGHT* PEOPLE.
HA HA!
BEEEEEP

HOW DO YOU THINK THEY MAKE SURE THE RIGHT PEOPLE ARE IN CHARGE?
DO THEY EVEN TRY?

SHOPS
AND WHAT ABOUT DECISIONS?
HOW DO THEY KNOW THEY'RE MAKING THE RIGHT CHOICE FOR THE COUNTRY?
WHAT IF OTHER PEOPLE DON'T LIKE THEIR DECISIONS? CAN THEY INFLUENCE WHAT THE RULERS DO?

WHO MAKES THE DECISIONS?

WHO CONTROLS WHERE THE MONEY GOES?

WHO DETERMINES RIGHT AND WRONG BEHAVIOR?

WHO PUNISHES PEOPLE WHO VIOLATE THE LAWS?

HOW DO THE RULERS COME TO POWER?

HOW DO THEY SET GOVERNMENT POLICIES?

HOW CAN REGULAR PEOPLE INFLUENCE WHAT THE RULERS DO?

Humans have experimented with several ways to rule with just a few.
DUTY FRE
Postcards

OLIG
This type of government can be recognized by some common signs...

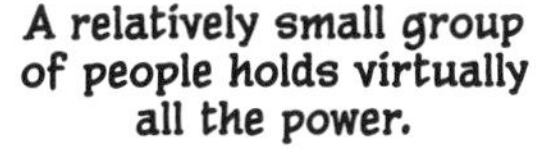

A relatively small group of people holds virtually all the power.

The members of that small group share key characteristics.

ARISTOCRACY

rule by birth

It's hard for other people to join the rulers' group, often because...

WARLORDISM

CELEBRATE MILITARY STRENGTH

...the members strictly control access to their group.

The best way to keep the club exclusive is by setting a high bar for membership.

Warlord's Lounge
If you want in, break down the door.

Theocracy Lounge
Open to ordained clergy; direct complaints and inquiries to your god.

Aristocracy Lounge
Please provide proof of birthright to enter.

Oligarchy Lounge
Show net worth to enter. Available for corporate sponsorship.

SEEMS LIKE THE GOAL ISN'T GETTING IN THE DOOR...

IT'S KEEPING OTHER PEOPLE OUT.

VIP
LOUNGE
AREA
THIS IS A PRIVATE CLUB. FOR MEMBERS ONLY.
BUT I JUST WANT TO KNOW WHAT THEY'RE DOING IN THERE!

I'M SORRY, MEMBERS' ACTIVITIES ARE CONFIDENTIAL.
RULES AND REGULATIONS ARE ONLY FOR MEMBERS.
CAN YOU AT LEAST TELL US WHAT THEY CAN AND CAN'T DO?

BUT...
NO, WAIT, HOW DO WE MAKE SURE THEY'RE FOLLOWING THE RULES?
DO I NEED TO CALL SECURITY?
COME ON.

TRAIN APPROACHING
MAYBE THERE'S ANOTHER WAY IN.

WHOOSH
OUR NEXT STOP IS: WARLORDISM.
WHOOOSH
I THOUGHT "WARLORD" WAS JUST ANOTHER WORD FOR "DICTATOR."
PLEASE HOLD ONTO THE HANDRAILS AS WE ENTER THE STATION.
WHOOSH SCREECH STOP
Like some dictators, warlords rule their territories through force and fear.
But where a dictator rules alone, *warlordism* happens when the central government collapses or loses its authority.
SLIDE
SLIDE
THE EMPEROR IS DEAD. LONG LIVE—
THIS PART IS MINE!
NO, MINE!
ME! MINE!
I'LL TAKE THIS, THANK YOU.
OH NO YOU DON'T!
In the power vacuum left behind, individual strongmen seize control of whatever they can.

Warlords are fundamentally *self-interested.* They look out for their own needs first and will do anything to stay on top.
THEN HOW DO THEY GET PEOPLE TO FOLLOW THEM?

They start with people who are already connected to them.
TROOPS, GIVE ME A HAND!

Then they keep their followers by mastering *patronage politics.*
WHISKEY
KEEP PULLING, MEN! I'LL MAKE IT WORTH YOUR WHILE!
THEY'RE RIPPING THE COUNTRY APART FOR NICE CARS AND ALCOHOL?

WHO DO YOU THINK CONTROLS ALL THE FOOD AND MEDICINE?
HAFTA FIGHT IF YOU WANNA EAT.
WE DON'T ALWAYS GET A CHOICE. THEY KIDNAPPED ME FROM SCHOOL.
IT'S CALLED CONSCRIPTION. NOW KEEP PULLING!

WARLORDS SOUND LIKE THE OPPOSITE OF GOVERNMENT.
HOW DO THEY GET ALL THAT FOOD AND MEDICINE AND THE FANCY CARS?
DO YOU HAVE TO BE REALLY RICH TO BE A WARLORD IN THE FIRST PLACE?
NOPE. ALL YOU NEED IS A FORCE STRONG ENOUGH TO CONTROL ***ECONOMIC LEVERAGE POINTS.***
Transportation networks,
extractive resource zones like mines and forests,
farmland that can grow cash crops like opium poppies, coffee, or coca,
and revenue hubs like checkpoints and tax offices.
BUT IF ALL THE REVENUE IS GOING TO THE WARLORDS,
WHO PAYS FOR STUFF LIKE ELECTRICITY, HEALTH CARE, PUBLIC SAFETY, SEWER SYSTEMS...
WHAT DO I GET OUT OF THOSE THINGS?
WELL, EVERYBODY BENEFITS FROM—
I'M STILL NOT HEARING ANYTHING ABOUT *ME*.

Within their territories, warlords are the absolute masters. They make all decisions, control all the wealth, and rarely allow others to gain influence.
SEEMS LIKE THE SPECIAL CHARACTERISTIC OF WARLORDS IS BEING A REAL JERK.
WRONG! STRENGTH IS WHAT MAKES A WARLORD!
YOU DO WHATEVER IT TAKES TO HOLD ONTO POWER!
DOES ANYONE HERE CARE ABOUT YOU?
ARE YOU KIDDING?
THEY BARELY REMEMBER WE EXIST.
THIS "GOVERNMENT" IS CAUSING MORE PROBLEMS THAN IT SOLVES.
LOOK AT THE MAP!
Countries fragment under warlord governance.
RIIIIIIIIIIIIIIP
Even if the borders remain intact, everything inside them is broken.

HA!
VICTORY IS
MINE!

AH, NEW
RECRUITS!
OH, NO!
WE'RE JUST...
TOURISTS?

WE DON'T
HAVE TOURISTS
HERE. WE HAVE
FOLLOWERS...
AND ENEMIES.

THAT'S...
SO...

WATCH
GAP
...LOOK, WHAT
A COINCIDENCE,
OUR TRAIN IS
LEAVING!

WHEW!
I USED TO THINK GOVERNMENT WAS SUPER BORING.
I USED TO THINK *AIRPORTS* WERE BORING.

OUR NEXT STOP IS: THEOCRACY.
THAT'S... A RELIGIOUS GOVERNMENT?

In a *theocracy,* religious hierarchy dictates how the government is organized and who can be a government official. Religious principles guide law and policy.
SO, LIKE, A GOVERNMENT WHERE MY PASTOR IS ALSO THE MAYOR?
OR IS IT A GOVERNMENT THAT DOES WHAT THE CLERGY TELLS IT TO DO?

Both kinds exist in the world today.
SOVEREIGN OF THE VATICAN CITY
SUPREME PONTIFF OF THE UNIVERSAL CHURCH
THE POPE?

HOW CAN ONE PERSON RUN A GOVERNMENT AND A CHURCH?
HIS HOLINESS WEARS MANY HATS. IN A MANNER OF SPEAKING.

HE CAN'T POSSIBLY DO EVERYTHING!
OF COURSE NOT! HE HAS PLENTY OF HELP.

AND THEY MAKE THE LAWS?
WITH APPROVAL FROM HIS HOLINESS, NATURALLY.
PONTIFICAL COMMISSION FOR THE VATICAN STATE
PRESIDENT OF THE PONTIFICAL COMMISSION
SUPREME TRIBUNAL OF THE APOSTOLIC SIGNATURA

The Vatican is small and almost everyone who lives there is a member of the Catholic Church. But not all theocracies look like that.
ST. PETER'S BASILICA

Sometimes lay officials run the day-to-day affairs of government, while certain religious authorities manage the big decisions behind the scenes.
PARLIAMENT OF IRAN

HOW CAN YOU RUN A GOVERNMENT IF OTHER PEOPLE ARE MAKING ALL THE DECISIONS?
Imagine a play. We see the actors, what they do, and how they interact.
I, THE PRESIDENT OF IRAN, CALL UPON YOU, THE ELECTED PARLIAMENT, TO TAKE ACTION...

But most of what we experience depends on the work of people behind the scenes.
PROPS

HM. AS SUPREME LEADER, I WANT ALL OF YOU TO MOVE TO THE RIGHT.

THE GUARDIANS' COUNCIL THINKS HE'S HAD THE SPOTLIGHT FOR LONG ENOUGH.
TIME TO REDIRECT THE PEOPLE'S ATTENTION.

SO WHO REALLY RUNS IRAN?
OH, IT'S SIMPLE...

THE AYATOLLAHS IN THE GUARDIANS' COUNCIL CHOOSE WHICH CLERICS CAN RUN FOR THE ASSEMBLY OF EXPERTS, WHICH PICKS AN AYATOLLAH TO BE SUPREME LEADER FOR LIFE, WHO APPOINTS THE GUARDIANS' COUNCIL, WHICH DECIDES WHO CAN RUN FOR PUBLIC OFFICE AND WHAT LAWS CAN BE PASSED...
I THOUGHT YOU SAID IT WAS SIMPLE.

THIS WHOLE PRESIDENT AND PARLIAMENT THING IS JUST FOR SHOW, THEN?
THEY TAKE CARE OF THE TEDIOUS BUREAUCRACY, AND WE KEEP THE POWER WHERE IT BELONGS.

WITH YOU?
WITH OUR INTERPRETATION OF GOD'S LAW, YOUNG LADY.

OKAY, OKAY, AND YOU MAKE DECISIONS BASED ON...
YOUR HOLY BOOK?
BASED ON FUNDAMENTAL RELIGIOUS PRINCIPLES.

FINE. AND SOMETIMES YOU CHOOSE LAYPEOPLE TO DO THE GRUNT WORK. WHY?

PEOPLE LOVE THE SPECTACLE OF ELECTIONS.
WHICH IS FINE, AS LONG AS WE CONTROL WHO CAN RUN. AND WHAT THEY DO ONCE THEY'RE IN OFFICE.

BUT IF THE LAY LEADERS DO WHAT THE CLERGY WANTS, AND THE CLERGY'S MAIN JOB IS MAKING SOCIETY CONFORM TO RELIGIOUS PRINCIPLES...
...THEN WHO THINKS ABOUT WHAT REGULAR PEOPLE WANT AND NEED?

THE FAITHFUL WILL HAVE ALL THEIR NEEDS MET BY LIVING IN THE VIRTUOUS ISLAMIC SOCIETY WE CREATE FOR THEM.
WHY WOULD WE VIOLATE OUR CATHOLIC PRINCIPLES JUST BECAUSE THE PEOPLE WANT SOMETHING DIFFERENT?

WATER
BUT HOLY BOOKS DON'T COVER A LOT OF THINGS MODERN PEOPLE NEED.
WHAT ABOUT PUBLIC TRANSIT? ACCESS TO ELECTRICITY AND CLEAN WATER? SAFE SCHOOLS?

AND WHAT IF THE CLERGY CAN'T AGREE ON WHAT RELIGIOUS PRINCIPLES TO FOLLOW?
THERE ARE A TON OF CHURCHES IN MY HOMETOWN:
CATHOLIC, METHODIST, LUTHERAN, PRESBYTERIAN, BAPTIST...
THEY'RE ALL CHRISTIAN, BUT THEY HAVE REALLY DIFFERENT IDEAS ABOUT WHAT THAT MEANS.

WE AVOID THAT PROBLEM BY NOT TOLERATING RELIGIOUS DISSENT.
OR POLITICAL DISSENT.
ANY DISAGREEMENT AT ALL, REALLY.
JUST BECAUSE YOU SILENCE DISSENT DOESN'T MEAN THAT WE CONSENT!
WE'RE TIRED OF THE ILLUSION OF DEMOCRACY! WE WANT THE REAL THING!
GREEN MOVEMENT
DEMOCRACY FOR IRAN
MY VOTE?
FREEDOM + DEMOCRACY IN IRAN
WHITE WEDNESDAYS

NONSENSE! RELIGIOUS GOVERNMENT UNITES PEOPLE ACROSS LANGUAGES AND CULTURES.
THEOCRACY IS THE ONLY WAY TO BUILD A RIGHTEOUS SOCIETY!

NOT TO MENTION HOW STABLE WE ARE.
LOOK AT THE VATICAN: STILL STANDING AFTER ALMOST TWO MILLENNIA. WHAT OTHER GOVERNMENT CAN SAY THAT?

THEY SOUND LIKE THOSE PHILOSOPHERS. OBSESSED WITH MAKING PEOPLE LIVE THE RIGHT WAY.
WE KNOW HOW GOD WANTS US TO LIVE. THAT'S WHY WE SHOULD BE IN CHARGE.
THEY MESS UP ALL THE TIME! THEY'RE HUMAN LIKE THE REST OF US!

THEY HAVE A POINT.
HOW DO YOUR CITIZENS HOLD YOU ACCOUNTABLE IF THEY DON'T LIKE WHAT YOUR GOVERNMENT DOES?
WE WILL ANSWER TO OUR GOD, THE ONLY ACCOUNTABILITY THAT REALLY MATTERS.
GREEN REVOLUTION
FREEDOM + DEMOCRACY IN IRAN
I DON'T AGREE! WHAT ABOUT THE SEXUAL ABUSE SCANDAL IN THE CATHOLIC CHURCH?
CHURCH LEADERS KNEW THOSE PRIESTS WERE DOING TERRIBLE THINGS, BUT THEY DIDN'T THROW THEM OUT OF THE PRIESTHOOD.
THEY JUST KEPT MOVING THEM TO NEW PLACES.
THEY DIDN'T STOP UNTIL THE PRESS UNCOVERED IT.
The Boston Globe
SCANDAL
Families win lawsuit
HOW DO YOU GET JUSTICE IF ALL THE OFFICIALS ARE IN FOR LIFE...
AND THERE ARE NO OUTSIDE INSTITUTIONS TO FORCE THEM TO DO THE RIGHT THING?
I'M NOT AUTHORIZED TO COMMENT ON THAT.
SEE? THIS IS EXACTLY WHY WE DON'T LET PEOPLE START DISAGREEING WITH US. WHERE WOULD IT END?!
SOUNDS LIKE THEOCRACIES ARE ULTIMATELY ABOUT SERVING THE CLERGY.
THESE "SPECIAL FEW" GOVERNMENTS REALLY AREN'T IMPRESSING ME SO FAR.

BUT DON'T YOU WANT RULERS WHO WILL PROTECT YOUR SOUL?
SORRY, *THESE* ARE THE COMMANDMENTS WE'RE LOOKING TO FOLLOW.

Lin & Julie's
IDEAL GOVERNMENT
• Predictable
• Fair
• Transparent

I HOPE WE'RE GETTING AWAY FROM RULERS WHO THINK THEY HAVE SOME SORT OF RIGHT TO BE IN CHARGE!
WELL, I HAVE GOOD NEWS AND BAD NEWS...
NEXT STOP ARISTOCRACY

I THOUGHT ARISTOCRATS ONLY EXISTED IN MEDIEVAL MONARCHIES.
THEY CAN BE A GOVERNMENT ALL BY THEMSELVES?
Aristocracy **is a type of government where rulers are chosen based on bloodlines and kinship.**

Their authority comes from owning a lot of land, leading a clan or tribe, or being the keeper of an important ritual.
BUT WHAT CAN ARISTOCRATS CONTRIBUTE TO GOVERNMENT TODAY?

A COUNTRY SHOULDN'T HAVE TO CHOOSE BETWEEN PROGRESS AND TRADITION.
SUCCESSFUL GOVERNMENTS FIND A WAY TO HONOR BOTH.

IN GHANA, OUR CONSTITUTION RECOGNIZES THE ARISTOCRACY AS ESSENTIAL.

ESSENTIAL HOW?
TRADITION SHAPES WHAT MY PEOPLE EXPECT OF THEIR LEADERS.

WE HAVE LIVED HERE FOR ALMOST A THOUSAND YEARS.
PART OF MY JOB AS CHIEF IS TO BE A CUSTODIAN OF OUR LAND AND OUR PEOPLE.
I MUST UNDERSTAND WHAT BOTH NEED TO THRIVE.
NOT JUST RIGHT NOW, BUT FOR THE NEXT GENERATION AND THE ONE AFTER THAT.

THE PERSON SITTING ON THIS STOOL DOESN'T ONLY MANAGE LAND AND LAW.
WHEN PEOPLE ARGUE, I USE OUR PRACTICES TO RESOLVE THEIR DISPUTES.
PEOPLE ACCEPT MY JUSTICE BECAUSE THEY UNDERSTAND WHERE IT COMES FROM.
THIS IS TRUE FOR MY TRIBE, AS IT IS TRUE FOR ALL OTHER TRIBES.

WHY DO THEY TRUST YOU WITH ALL THIS POWER?
MY FATHER SAT ON THIS STOOL BEFORE ME, AND HIS UNCLE BEFORE HIM.

OH, YOU WERE BORN TO THE RIGHT FAMILY?
NOT ONLY THAT.

THE QUEEN MOTHERS CHOSE ME AS THE MOST WORTHY CANDIDATE.

WE ONLY CHOOSE FROM AMONG THE FIRST FAMILY THAT CALLED THIS PLACE HOME.
WE ALSO GUIDE SOCIAL AND ECONOMIC DEVELOPMENT, ANTICIPATING THE FUTURE NEEDS OF OUR PEOPLE.

SO AN ARISTOCRACY IS ABOUT RULING FOR THE GREATER GOOD?
LIKE ARISTOTLE SAID?
TO BE A QUEEN MOTHER MEANS LOOKING AFTER THE WHOLE COMMUNITY.

I'M ONE OF TEN THOUSAND QUEEN MOTHERS WORKING TOGETHER ACROSS GHANA.
AND I SIT IN THE HOUSE OF CHIEFS IN PARLIAMENT.

Each aristocracy distributes power in its own way, while keeping it all in the family.

WHY ARE THEY SO OBSESSED WITH BLOODLINES?
Aristocracy rests on some big assumptions.

WE HAVE AN INNATE GRASP OF THE RIGHT WAY TO LIVE.
SOME PEOPLE ARE JUST MEANT TO RULE.

THAT SOUNDS SUSPICIOUSLY LIKE THAT VIRTUOUS RULER STUFF.
PRECISELY! IT'S ALL IN THE VIRTUES.

A TRUE ARISTOCRAT HAS A CERTAIN... MAGNITUDE OF SOUL.
OKAY, I'LL BITE: WHAT GIVES YOU "MAGNITUDE OF SOUL"?
WE'RE SO GLAD YOU ASKED.

WISDOM
BENIFICENCE
Prudence
Decorum
JUSTICE

I AGREE THAT RULERS SHOULD BE EDUCATED, PUBLIC-SPIRITED, REASONABLE...
BUT A LOT OF PEOPLE HAVE THESE QUALITIES, NO MATTER WHO THEIR PARENTS ARE.
Polite

SO WHY CAN'T ANYONE WITH THOSE QUALITIES RULE?
WHAT YOU HAVE TO UNDERSTAND IS THAT SOME PEOPLE ARE JUST SUPERIOR.

FACE FACTS: YOU COMMONERS HAVEN'T A CLUE HOW TO HANDLE OUR WEALTH AND POWER.
IT ISN'T YOUR FAULT, YOU SIMPLY DON'T HAVE THE *JE NE SAIS QUOI*.

SO HOW DO YOU GET YOUR SUPER-DUPER SPECIAL ABILITIES?
EYE ROLL
MAYBE SHE'S BORN WITH IT...
...MAYBE IT'S HOW HE WAS RAISED.

YOU KNOW WHAT? I DON'T THINK I NEED TO SEE MORE.
RUDE.

YOU KNOW, FOR A MINUTE I THOUGHT I COULD SEE THE POINT OF AN ARISTOCRACY.
AT LEAST THE PART ABOUT HAVING PROGRESS WITHOUT SACRIFICING TRADITION.
WATCH GAP
REALLY?

I MEAN, OKAY, SO I GREW UP IN A SMALL WISCONSIN TOWN. NOW I LIVE IN A CITY IN VIRGINIA.
I LIKE BOTH PLACES, BUT, BOY, DO PEOPLE HAVE DIFFERENT IDEAS ABOUT GOVERNMENT.

I DON'T MEAN WHAT POLITICAL PARTY YOU BELONG TO.
OVER OUR HISTORIES, GOVERNMENT HAS MEANT REALLY DIFFERENT THINGS TO VIRGINIANS THAN IT HAS TO WISCONSINITES.

YOU KNOW, WISCONSIN: HOME OF INDEPENDENT PIONEER FARMERS!
AND VIRGINIA: HOME OF JEFFERSON AND WASHINGTON!
BUT ALSO HOME TO A LOT OF PEOPLE WHO ACT LIKE THE CIVIL WAR JUST ENDED.
I DON'T THINK OUR GOVERNMENT IS ALWAYS GOOD AT REMEMBERING HOW DIFFERENTLY PEOPLE SEE THINGS AROUND THE COUNTRY.
DOES THE GOVERNMENT NEED TO KEEP THOSE DIFFERENT VISIONS ALIVE?
THE CIVIL WAR ENDED MORE THAN 150 YEARS AGO. ISN'T IT TIME TO MOVE ON?
FOR SURE, BUT THAT'S EASIER SAID THAN DONE. I THINK THE U.S. COULD USE LEADERS TO HELP US BRIDGE THAT GAP.
HOW?
WELL, UM...
MY GRAMMA IS ALWAYS TALKING ABOUT HOW—
"POLITICAL CORRECTNESS" IS AN ATTACK ON OUR CULTURE!
SHE DOESN'T UNDERSTAND WHY PEOPLE ARE CHANGING THE WAY THEY TALK AND BEHAVE.

I THINK IF THERE WAS SOME LEADER SHE ALREADY TRUSTED, THEY WOULD HELP HER SEE THAT CHANGE ISN'T ALWAYS THREATENING.
SOMEONE LIKE THE CHIEF IN GHANA, WHO WAS ALREADY A ROLE MODEL FOR HOW TO LIVE.
WHY DO WE NEED ARISTOCRATS FOR THAT? COULDN'T POLITICIANS OR YOUR PASTOR BE THAT FOR HER?
I GUESS. BUT ARISTOCRATS REPRESENT THE OLD TRADITIONS...

DON'T THEY MAKE CHANGE SEEM LESS THREATENING BY STICKING AROUND?
THAT'S INTERESTING. I HADN'T THOUGHT OF IT THAT WAY.

I DON'T KNOW. I'M PROBABLY WRONG.
WHAT DO YOU THINK?
IF THERE'S ONE THING WE'VE LEARNED SO FAR, IT'S THAT EVERYONE IS PROBABLY WRONG.

I SEE IT DIFFERENTLY, THOUGH.
MY FAMILY MOVED TO THE U.S. FROM SHANGHAI WHEN I WAS A LITTLE GIRL. WE DIDN'T FEEL LIKE WE BELONGED FOR A LONG TIME.
WE DIDN'T SPEAK ENGLISH, NONE OF THE FOOD OR HOLIDAYS WERE FAMILIAR, AND THERE WERE PLENTY OF PEOPLE WHO WENT OUT OF THEIR WAY TO MAKE US FEEL UNWELCOME.

WE TRIED TO LEARN HOW TO BE "GOOD AMERICANS" AND FIT IN. BUT CALIFORNIA PASSED ENGLISH-ONLY LAWS AND ELECTED NATIVISTS.
VOTERS USED INSTITUTIONS OF GOVERNMENT TO TELL US WE COULD NEVER BELONG.

BUT THE LONGER WE LIVED HERE, THE MORE WE SAW THERE ISN'T ONE RIGHT WAY TO BE AN AMERICAN.
IN FACT, WHAT IT MEANS TO BE AMERICAN IS ALWAYS CHANGING.

UNDERSTANDING THAT HELPED MY FAMILY FIND A WAY TO LIVE THAT INCLUDES OUR WHOLE STORY.
BOTH GOVERNMENT AND SOCIETY HAVE A SAY IN WHETHER PEOPLE FEEL LIKE THEY BELONG.
WE FORMED COALITIONS TO ELECT NEW PEOPLE AND REVERSE MANY OF THOSE RACIST LAWS.
BUT THERE ARE STILL PLENTY OF PEOPLE WHO DON'T SEE US AS AMERICAN.

I DON'T THINK TRADITIONAL ARISTOCRATIC LEADERS WOULD HAVE HELPED US FEEL WELCOME.
WHY?
YOU WERE SAYING ABOUT GOVERNMENT MEANING DIFFERENT THINGS TO PEOPLE IN WISCONSIN AND VIRGINIA?

WELL... GOVERNMENT HAS MEANT VERY DIFFERENT THINGS TO THE WHITE PEOPLE AND THE PEOPLE OF COLOR IN EACH OF THOSE PLACES.
WHOSE VISION OF AMERICA WOULD THE ARISTOCRATS BE PRESERVING?

OH. YEAH. I DIDN'T THINK ABOUT THAT.
OUR NEXT STOP IS: OLIGARCHY.
OLLY... OLIG... WHAT?
I DON'T KNOW THIS ONE, EITHER.
An *oligarchy* is a government where power comes from wealth.
IT'S JUST ABOUT BEING RICH?
BUT AREN'T ARISTOCRATS RICH, TOO? THEY HAVE ALL THOSE FANCY HOUSES.
In an aristocracy, wealth usually means how much land you own.
In an oligarchy—
CASH, CASH, MONEY, BABY! WE GOT IT, WE'RE GONNA KEEP IT!
HUH, RICH PEOPLE RUNNING THE COUNTRY. SOUNDS A BIT FAMILIAR, DOESN'T IT?
I *THOUGHT* SO.
BUT AMERICA'S A DEMOCRACY, NOT AN OLIGARCHY. RIGHT?

In an oligarchy, a relatively small group of extremely wealthy people control a disproportionate amount of political power.
Sometimes they hold positions in government.
YOU TELL HIM HE CAN HAVE HIS LICENSE WHEN HE MAKES A DONATION...
LET'S BUY THAT TV STATION....
MINISTER OF PUBLIC WORKS
YES, MY FACTORY WILL SUPPLY THE HOSPITAL...
THE ROADS CONTRACT GOES TO MY COMPANY, MIKHAIL...
PUT ME ON THE COVER OF *PHILANTHROPY TODAY!*
Sometimes they work from behind the scenes.
HERE'S THAT MEMO ON LEGAL LOOPHOLES IN ANTITRUST LAW.
DID YOU CALL—
—YOUR BROTHER-IN-LAW ON THE FCC?
YOU'RE HAVING DINNER WITH HIM TONIGHT.
THE DEMOCRATS ARE ON LINE 2, REPUBLICANS ON LINE 3.
SIR, YOU'VE BEEN INVITED TO SIT ON THE PRESIDENT'S BLUE RIBBON COMMISSION ON OUR FISCAL FUTURE.

Oligarchs use their control over the government to grow their wealth and to protect it from competitors and even the government itself.
HE'S TOO MUCH TROUBLE, MIKHAIL! ARREST HIM.
MY TV STATION WILL REPORT HE'S UNDER INVESTIGATION FOR CORRUPTION.
SENATOR FRISK, THANK YOU FOR PUTTING THAT LITTLE AMENDMENT IN THE TAX BILL.
WHEN AM I TAKING YOU AND THE FAMILY TO MY CHALET AGAIN?
IF ALL THEY CARE ABOUT IS BEING RICH, WHY BOTHER WITH THE GOVERNMENT?
WHY NOT JUST KEEP THEIR MONEY UNDER A MATTRESS?
Wealth isn't only hard cash. It can be real estate, contracts, licenses for communication networks, patents on lifesaving drugs...
Oligarchs use government to control how they make future money.
THESE WOMEN ARE BORING ME, TAKE THEM AWAY!
WHAT ABOUT ALL THE PARTS OF GOVERNMENT THAT AREN'T ABOUT MAKING MONEY?
YOU KNOW, THE STUFF REGULAR PEOPLE RELY ON?

The truth is, oligarchs rarely see the challenges regular people face.
IS THAT POSSIBLE? WE ALL LIVE IN THE SAME COUNTRY.
NOT REALLY. WE SEE IT IN THE BAY AREA, WHERE I LIVE.
SLAM
NO ENTRY
ALL THE RICHEST PEOPLE LIVE IN GATED COMMUNITIES AND SEND THEIR KIDS TO PRIVATE SCHOOLS.
THEY BELONG TO COUNTRY CLUBS AND YACHT CLUBS NO ONE ELSE CAN AFFORD...
THEY NEVER TAKE PUBLIC TRANSPORTATION...
THEY EVEN HAVE THEIR OWN PRIVATE PARKS.
THEY NEVER ACTUALLY SEE REGULAR PEOPLE, UNLESS WE'RE CLEANING THEIR HOUSES OR CATERING THEIR PARTIES.
YOU WOULD NOT BELIEVE HOW LONG WE HAD TO SIT IN TRAFFIC TO GET HERE TONIGHT!
WHAT'S WRONG WITH THIS CITY?
WE TOOK THE HELICOPTER!

Oligarchs also have an easier time getting the government's ear.
THERE WERE PEOPLE WALKING ALL OVER THE FREEWAY.
IT LOOKED LIKE ONE OF *THOSE* PROTESTS.

IT SHOULD BE ILLEGAL TO BLOCK THE ROADS LIKE THAT.
I'M SURE THEY'RE UPSET, BUT THEY SHOULDN'T BE ALLOWED TO GET IN THE WAY.

DO YOU KNOW HOW MANY OF MY TRUCKS ARE DELAYED RIGHT NOW?
YOU KNOW WHAT THEY SAY: CALL YOUR REPRESENTATIVE!

OH, CONGRESSMAN!
WHAT CAN I DO FOR YOU?
THAT'S CERTAINLY NOT HOW IT WORKS FOR THE REST OF US.
THERE'S A BIG DIFFERENCE BETWEEN WRITING AN EMAIL AND HAVING YOUR REPRESENTATIVE RIGHT IN YOUR LIVING ROOM.

Oligarchs also use their wealth and power to control the political agenda.
THAT SOUNDS LIKE A CONSPIRACY THEORY THING.
A *political agenda* is a list of issues that leaders intend to address using the power of the government.
Our personal political agendas are based on what we need and what impacts our communities.
AM I STILL GOING TO HAVE A JOB NEXT YEAR?
WHAT IF ONE OF US GETS SICK? HOW WILL WE PAY FOR HER COLLEGE?
Allen Family Agenda: Jobs, Paid Sick Leave, Student Debt
Political parties adopt a political agenda they'll work on together if elected.
Public Safety
Climate Crisis
Immigration
Jobs for the 21st Century
Drug Prices
Privacy
TOGETHER, WE CAN BE THE CHANGE WE WANT TO SEE IN THE WORLD!

Oligarchs influence both agendas. They control which issues receive attention through the media outlets and other information sources they own.
GLOBAL NEWS
JOBS FLEEING OVERSEAS

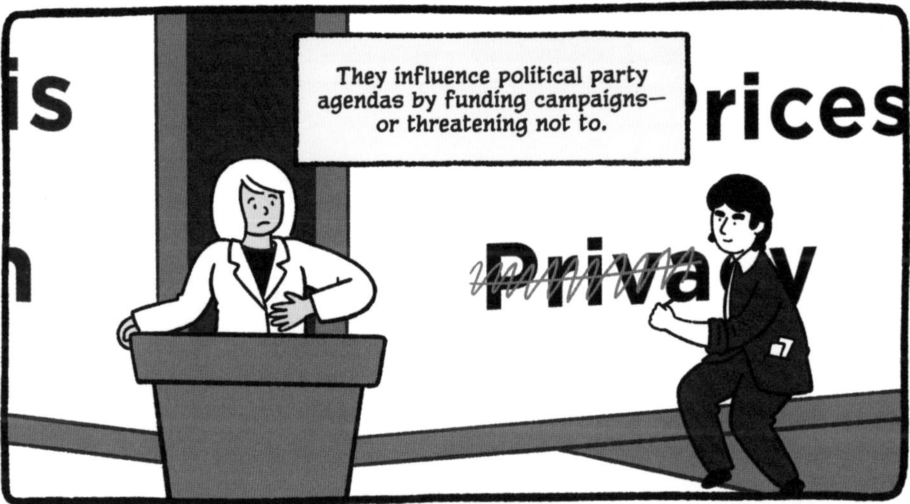
They influence political party agendas by funding campaigns—or threatening not to.
Prices
Privacy

THIS IS SOUNDING MORE AND MORE FAMILIAR.

WHOO

WHOOOOO
WHAT'S *THAT?!*

The Gilded Age was a time of immense change in America:

the end of Reconstruction and the reimposition of white rule throughout the South,

new people arriving from around the globe,

fierce debates about whether the dollar should be backed by gold or silver,

smoke-filled back rooms, corruption, identity politics, and the rise of corporations.

VANDERBILT RAILROAD
CARNEGIE STEEL
STANFORD
THE ROBBER BARONS!

SUCH A DISTASTEFUL PHRASE.
WE PREFER "CAPTAINS OF INDUSTRY."

WE INVENTED MODERN AMERICA.
BY RUNNING A BIG COMPANY?

DON'T MAKE IT SOUND SO PETTY. WE CHANGED THE WORLD!
WE LAID TRACKS ACROSS THE UNTAMED WILDERNESS!
WE DREW TREASURE FROM THE VERY BOWELS OF THE EARTH!
I'M SORRY, WHO LAID TRACKS?
KOFF
KOFF
DIDN'T SEE...YOU... DOWN THERE... GETTING BLACK LUNG...

...IN OTHER WORDS, WE BUILT THE AMERICAN ECONOMIC JUGGERNAUT!

HI. THE ENTIRE WORKING CLASS WOULD LIKE A WORD.

YOUR "JUGGERNAUT" RAN RIGHT OVER OUR DIGNITY, SAFETY, AND BASIC HUMAN RIGHTS!

The oligarchs of the Gilded Age thought certain qualities made them special.

And they did have a lot of things in common, like being:
WHITE
MALE
PROTESTANT
BORN INTO UPPER-MIDDLE-CLASS FAMILIES
AND WELL EDUCATED.
WHAT MATTERS IS THAT WE'RE MEN OF CHARACTER. HARD WORK AND VIRTUOUS LIVING IS WHAT MADE US RICH AND POWERFUL.
INITIATIVE!
PERSEVERANCE!
SOBRIETY!
FRUGALITY!
I'M CONFUSED. CAN'T YOU HAVE BIG COMPANIES ***AND*** DEMOCRACY?
WHAT MADE THE GILDED AGE AN OLIGARCHY?
Until the end of the Civil War, most people worked for themselves or as part of a family business.

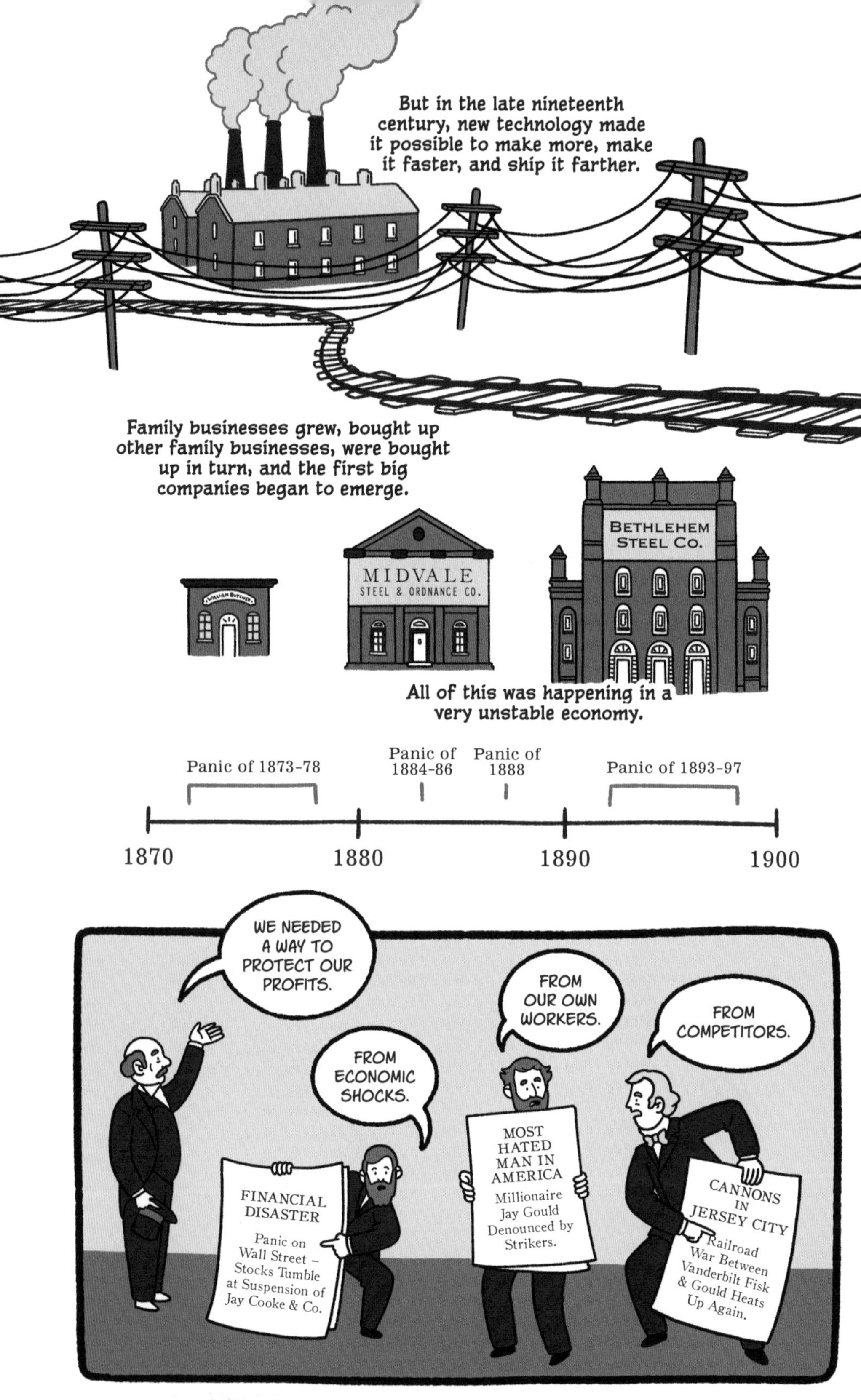

But in the late nineteenth century, new technology made it possible to make more, make it faster, and ship it farther.
Family businesses grew, bought up other family businesses, were bought up in turn, and the first big companies began to emerge.
MIDVALE
STEEL & ORDNANCE CO.
BETHLEHEM STEEL CO.
All of this was happening in a very unstable economy.
Panic of 1873-78
Panic of 1884-86
Panic of 1888
Panic of 1893-97
1870
1880
1890
1900
WE NEEDED A WAY TO PROTECT OUR PROFITS.
FROM ECONOMIC SHOCKS.
FROM OUR OWN WORKERS.
FROM COMPETITORS.
FINANCIAL DISASTER
Panic on Wall Street – Stocks Tumble at Suspension of Jay Cooke & Co.
MOST HATED MAN IN AMERICA
Millionaire Jay Gould Denounced by Strikers.
CANNONS IN JERSEY CITY
Railroad War Between Vanderbilt Fisk & Gould Heats Up Again.

BROUGHT TO YOU BY
THE STANDARD OIL COMPANY

ROCKEFELLER'S RULES
FOR BUILDING A TRUST

1. **Form a board of directors to control all your companies.** Cut down on overhead!

2. **Convince your rivals to join.** Why have competition when you can have shareholders?

3. **Fix prices and quotas.** Enrich your friends, bankrupt your enemies!

4. Why not **buy your whole supply chain** while you're at it?

5. **Profit!**

The bigger the companies got, the more influence each one had on how America functioned. No industry was as big and influential as the railroads.
MEAT
GRAIN
COAL
IF YOU WANT TO MAKE IT IN AMERICA, YOU NEED ACCESS TO THE RAILWAYS.
GRAIN
In theory, there were standard rates for hauling freight.
BUT ALL THE FAT CATS NEGOTIATE DISCOUNTS WITH EACH OTHER...
WHILE US LITTLE GUYS PAY THROUGH THE NOSE.
GRAIN
GRAIN
LOOK, LITTLE MAN, IT'S JUST NATURAL SELECTION BY THE MARKETS.
SORRY, WHAT WERE YOU SAYING?
I WANT A DISCOUNT ON *ALL* STANDARD OIL SHIPMENTS.
AND IN EXCHANGE, STANDARD OIL WILL ONLY SHIP ON OUR LINES.
SINCE WE REFINE ALMOST 90% OF THE COUNTRY'S OIL, THAT'S QUITE A CONTRACT.
It was a system that worked for everyone who was already making money, but not for anybody else.

Railroads got guaranteed business. Their customers weren't shopping around.
Corporations got to keep their costs down...and keep their competition from getting special rates, too.
Businesses got bigger and bigger. For the first time, single corporations were controlling most of what America consumed, and more and more people were working for these big companies.

EVERY DAY IT'S LONGER HOURS, HIGHER QUOTAS, AND CRUELER BOSSES.
I DON'T FEEL LIKE I HAVE ANY CONTROL OVER MY LIFE ANYMORE.
SOMEONE HAS TO STEP IN OR WE'LL BE WORKED TO DEATH!

OH, LIKE THE GOVERNMENT?
THE WHO?
WHY DID YOU HAVE TO SAY THAT?
The government had never been very involved in regulating commercial activity, and the new industrialists weren't interested in changing that.

People wanted the government to solve two big problems. The first: what to do about the railroads? The oligarchs used every lever they had to make sure they came out on top.

They put their own people on the Supreme Court and state courts, too. And, of course, they had another powerful way to influence government officials.
WE'RE ALL FRIENDS! DRINKS FOR MY FRIENDS!

THESE DAYS, ALL I HEAR FROM MY CONSTITUENTS IS "REGULATE RAILROAD RATES!"
DO YOU SAY THESE THINGS JUST TO HURT ME?

YOU KNOW US. WE WENT TO SCHOOL TOGETHER. OUR CHILDREN HAVE MARRIED EACH OTHER.
WHAT HAVE YOUR VOTERS EVER DONE FOR YOU?

When a commission was finally established to regulate the railroads, the oligarchs undermined it.

TODAY, I SIGN INTO LAW THE INTERSTATE COMMERCE ACT OF 1887!
IT SAYS THE RAILROADS HAVE TO CHARGE "REASONABLE RATES."
WHAT DOES "REASONABLE" MEAN?

THE ICC CAN DETERMINE WHETHER AN ESTABLISHED RATE IS REASONABLE...
...BUT IT CAN'T SET THE RATE ITSELF.

SO WE HAVE TO GO TO COURT EVERY TIME WE THINK THE RATES ARE UNFAIR?
WHO HAS THE MONEY OR TIME FOR THAT?
WE DO...

Even some railroad owners saw the problem.
"THIS ENORMOUS BUSINESS IS NOW IN THE CONTROL OF SEVERAL HUNDRED PETTY CHIEFTAINS...
"WHO ARE PRACTICALLY INDEPENDENT SOVEREIGNS...
"EXERCISING FUNCTIONS AND PREROGATIVES IN DEFIANCE OF THE LAWS...
"AND PRACTICALLY DENYING THEIR AMENABILITY TO THE LAWS OF THE COUNTRY."
ST. Paul RAILROAD
THE ONLY PROBLEM IS THAT YOU THINK THAT'S A PROBLEM.

The directors of other big corporations supported the railroads all the way.
WHY WOULD THEY DO THAT?
IF WE LET THEM REGULATE SHIPPING RATES, WHO KNOWS WHAT THEY'LL DO NEXT. END MONOPOLIES?
In fact, monopolies were the government's second big problem.
MR. ROCKEFELLER, SIR...
ALL THESE STATES PASSED LAWS SAYING OUR OIL HAS TO BE INSPECTED.
IS THAT SO? GET THOSE SAFETY INSPECTORS ON OUR PAYROLL IMMEDIATELY.
The federal and state governments tried to regulate Standard Oil for decades.
SHERMAN ANTITRUST ACT
prohibiting every contract, conbination, or conspiracy in restraint of trade monopolization, attempted monopolization, or conspiracy or combination to monopolize
THAT WENT ABOUT AS WELL AS YOU'D EXPECT.
Congress passed the Sherman Antitrust Act in 1890 to break up monopolies such as Standard Oil and the railroad consortiums.

The oligarchs used their influence over Congress and the courts to derail enforcement of the new act.
THIS ACT DOESN'T APPLY TO *MANUFACTURING*, JUST COMMERCE.
YOU GO ON PRODUCING 98% OF THE SUGAR IN THE COUNTRY.
THE SHERMAN ACT SAYS LABOR UNIONS CAN BE AN ILLEGAL CONSPIRACY.
THAT MEANS NO MORE STRIKES OR BOYCOTTS, YOU TROUBLEMAKERS.
JANUARY 1895
SUGAR TRUST CASE
FEBRUARY 1908
DANBURY HATTERS' CASE

SO THE ONLY PEOPLE WHO GOT REGULATED WERE WORKERS?
NOW YOU SEE WHY WE'RE SO ANGRY!
THAT'S GROSS!
BUT IT'S NOT LIKE THAT NOW, RIGHT?
SO HOW DID WE FIX IT?
Some agencies were created to better regulate corporate behavior, like the Federal Communications Commission and Federal Trade Commission.

But better isn't fixed.
We don't have oil monopolies anymore. But just a few corporations own basically all our internet and communications infrastructure.
Some of the big Gilded Age corporations, like General Electric, are still doing just fine.
DOESN'T THE FEDERAL GOVERNMENT KEEP THEM FROM DOING THE REALLY BAD STUFF?
DOES IT?

LOOK AT WHO SITS ON THE FCC AND THE FTC: FORMER CORPORATE EXECUTIVES.
WHO'S REALLY MAKING DECISIONS IF THE CORPORATIONS CONTROL THE REGULATORS?
OR WHAT ABOUT BUYING POLITICIANS? THE SUPREME COURT RULED IN *CITIZENS UNITED* THAT CAMPAIGN CONTRIBUTIONS COUNT AS FREE SPEECH.
WEALTHY BUSINESSMEN STILL INFLUENCE WHO GETS ELECTED.
TO TRAMS
The historian Nell Irvin Painter described the Gilded Age in words that could also describe America today.
"Capitalism makes some people really rich and democracy is not strong enough to counter the power of great wealth. Capitalism helps a lot of people in a lot of ways. Capitalists aren't just robber barons and the very rich. It's not all bad, but it's very powerful."
BUT THAT MEANS...THE OLIGARCHS ARE WEARING OUR DEMOCRACY LIKE A DISGUISE?
I WANT OUR DEMOCRACY TO BE REAL. BUT I ALSO DON'T WANT TO BE FOOLED BY A SHINY EXTERIOR.
SO WHAT DO WE DO?
MAYBE LEARNING A LITTLE MORE ABOUT DEMOCRACY WILL GIVE US SOME IDEAS.
The GOVERNMENT Bistro
Try the Rule by Many!
TERMINAL 3

YEAH. GOOD IDEA.

ATTENTION PASSENGERS:
FLIGHT 5694 HAS BEEN DELAYED TWO HOURS. I REPEAT...
TRAIN DEPARTING

ANOTHER DELAY?

WHAT ARE YOU WATCHING OUT THERE?
HM?

OH, I WAS JUST THINKING ABOUT THE PLANES.
DON'T WORRY. WE'RE DELAYED BUT WE WON'T MISS THANKSGIVING.

NO, IT'S NOT THAT!
I WAS THINKING ABOUT ALL THE DIFFERENT KINDS OF GOVERNMENT, AND WHAT IF THEY WERE PLANES?

I BEG YOUR PARDON?

I MEAN, WHAT IF THAT PLANE WAS RUN LIKE A *MONARCHY?*

THERE'D BE ONE PILOT FOR LIFE AND WE'D JUST HAVE TO HOPE THEY DO A GOOD JOB.
I WISH HIS MAJESTY WOULD PUT THE ENGINES BACK ON.
IN A *DICTATORSHIP,* THE ONLY THING THAT MATTERED WOULD BE WHO CONTROLLED THE COCKPIT.
THIS IS YOUR GLORIOUS CAPTAIN SPEAKING.
IF YOU WANT TO LIVE, THEN THROW ALL THOSE OTHER PILOTS OUT OF THE PLANE!
WARLORDS WOULD WANT THE PLANE ONLY FOR ITS PARTS.
THE PLANE IS MINE.
THE SLIDES ARE MINE.
THE LIFE JACKETS ARE MINE.
THE LUGGAGE IS MINE.
THE OXYGEN MASKS ARE MINE.

TRAINING WOULD BE LESS IMPORTANT IN A *THEOCRACY* THAN COMPLYING WITH SCRIPTURE.

IN THE EVENT OF A SUDDEN LOSS OF CABIN PRESSURE, OXYGEN MASKS WILL DROP FOR THE VIRTUOUS AND WORTHY.

THE HOLY BOOK SAYS NOTHING ABOUT SEAT BELTS, MA'AM.

IN AN *ARISTOCRACY*, ALL OF FIRST CLASS WOULD BELIEVE THEY WERE BORN KNOWING HOW TO FLY.

BUT WHO'S FLYING THE PLANE *RIGHT NOW?*

I JUST REALLY *GET* FLYING, YOU KNOW?

PILOTS HAVE BEEN IN MY FAMILY FOR GENERATIONS.

I SEE WHAT YOU'RE GETTING AT. SOME OF THOSE PLANES WOULDN'T FLY WELL—
—OR AT ALL.

I WOULDN'T WANT TO BE ON ANY OF THEM.

IS IT TOO MUCH TO ASK FOR COMPETENT PEOPLE WHO CARE IF THE REGULAR PASSENGERS LIVE OR DIE?
I HOPE NOT.
PUSH

RULE BY MANY
FORTUNATELY, WE HAVE ONE MORE OPTION.

We the
People

We the
People

Democracies differ from other governments in many ways.
But the first thing you notice is all the people.
WHOA.
THERE'S SO MUCH GOING ON.
IS DEMOCRACY A GOVERNMENT OF EVERYONE YELLING AT EVERYONE ELSE?
Dialogue is the heart of democracy. But democracy is more than a lot of talk.
OKAY...
VOTE
TOWN HALL
MEETING TODAY
We the People
SIGN OUR PETITION
OFFICIAL ELECTION BALLOT
WHAT ELSE GOES INTO DEMOCRACY?
I DON'T THINK I COULD EXPLAIN IT. EVEN TO MYSELF.

DO YOU THINK EVERYONE HERE KNOWS WHAT DEMOCRACY IS?
THEY ALL LOOK LIKE THEY DO.
I FEEL LIKE EVERYONE KNOWS MORE THAN ME WHEN IT COMES TO THIS STUFF.

SO WHAT'S THE ANSWER?
WHAT'S THE DEFINITION OF DEMOCRACY?
There isn't one.

Not only one.

Human beings have been experimenting with democracy for more than two thousand years.
THAT'S A LONG EXPERIMENT.

But we've never settled on just one way to give power to the people.
THAT CAN'T BE RIGHT. LET ME LOOK THIS UP.

WELL?
I GOT 300 ***MILLION*** RESULTS.

I DON'T BELIEVE IT! WE CAME ALL THIS WAY TO FIND OUT WE CAN'T EVEN DEFINE IT?
SOMEONE TELL ME WHAT DEMOCRACY MEANS!

AHEM.

EQUALITY!
I CAN DO WHATEVER I WANT!
VOTING!
THE GOVERNMENT WORKS FOR US, NOT THE OTHER WAY AROUND!
EVERYONE HAS THE POWER TO CHANGE THINGS.
FREEDOM!
MY OPINION IS JUST AS IMPORTANT AS ANYONE'S.
NO ONE CAN TAKE MY RIGHTS AWAY!
WE CAN DISAGREE, BUT WORK TOGETHER.

Democracy means very different things to different people.

History, culture, and values shapes how we perceive people,

what we think our government should look like,

and how we balance our freedoms with others' rights.

BUT THEN HOW DO YOU KNOW YOU'RE GETTING THE RIGHT BALANCE?

It's like building your perfect burger. Each democracy starts with the same ingredients but puts them together in its own special way.

CITIZENS AS PART OF DECISION-MAKING

PARTICIPATION IN GOVERNMENT VIA VOTING, PETITIONS, RUNNING FOR OFFICE

LEADERS WHO RULE BY CONSENT OF CITIZENS

PEACEFUL COMPETITION FOR POWER

The GOVERNMENT Bistro

ACCESS TO DIVERSE SOURCES OF INFORMATION

THERE MUST BE A SECRET SAUCE TO HOLD THEM ALL TOGETHER.

Of course, the most basic ingredient in any democracy is citizens.
BECAUSE WE VOTE, RIGHT?

"Voter" is only one of the hats citizens wear in a democracy.
AIRPORT APPAREL CO
Democratic governments rely on networks of dialogue and cooperation to make decisions.

WE CHOOSE REPRESENTATIVES–
–AND WE *ARE* THE REPRESENTATIVES.
VOTER
REP

WE TELL OUR GOVERNMENT WHAT IT SHOULD BE WORKING ON.
OR SHINE A LIGHT ON WHAT'S BEEN OVERLOOKED.
POLITICAL ORGANIZER

WE KEEP INFORMATION FLOWING IN EVERY DIRECTION.
NEWS!

CITIZENS ARE THE EXPERTS, TOO.
BECAUSE OF OUR EDUCATION AND TRAINING, OR OUR LIFE EXPERIENCE.
EXPERT

THE OTHER TYPES OF GOVERNMENT DIDN'T PRIORITIZE DIALOGUE AND COOPERATION.

VIP LOUNGE AREA

IT'S PRETTY DIFFERENT.

BUT I BET WE HAVE THE SAME QUESTION.

IF PEOPLE HAVE ALL THESE DIFFERENT ROLES—

—AND EVERYONE HAS THEIR OWN NOTION OF DEMOCRACY—

—HOW DO WE EVER AGREE ON ANYTHING?

SEEMS LIKE WE'RE BACK TO EVERYONE YELLING AT EACH OTHER FOREVER.
RPORT APPAR
Humans have been debating that question for more than 2,500 years.

In fact, since the ancient—
DON'T SAY IT.
OH NO, NOT AGAIN.

ahem Since the ancient philosophers—
DID YOU MISS US?
WE'RE BAAACK!
HOW CAN WE ENLIGHTEN YOU?
WE WERE TRYING TO FIGURE OUT HOW TO HAVE DEMOCRACY WITHOUT FIGHTING ALL THE TIME.

SEE, SOCRATES? THIS IS MY EXACT POINT.
THE ONLY WAY TO TRULY AVOID CONFLICT IS IF ALL THE DECISION-MAKERS THINK THE SAME WAY.
BUT DEMOCRACY IS ALL ABOUT EMBRACING DIVERSE OPINIONS.

THAT IS THE FAST LANE TO CHAOSTOWN.
IF YOU WANT TO AVOID CONFLICT, YOU HAVE TO LIMIT POWER TO A FEW GOOD MEN.

YOU GOTTA CULTIVATE THE WHOLE VIRTUOUS LIFESTYLE!
TRAIN 'EM FROM BABIES TO THINK OF THE INDIVIDUAL, SOCIETY, AND GOVERNMENT AS ONE THING!
ENGINEER LITTLE VIRTUOUS RULER MACHINES!
CALM DOWN, PLATO.

OOOKAY...
MAYBE WE SHOULD JUST ASK SOMEONE ELSE.

BUMP

THEIR PROBLEM IS THEY THINK CONFLICT *IS* A PROBLEM.
WHAT?
UGH, NOT DEMOCRITUS AND FRIENDS.

POLITICAL CONFLICT ISN'T A BAD THING AS LONG AS IT'S MANAGED RIGHT.

CONFLICT CHALLENGES THE STATUS QUO. IT TESTS IDEAS AND SEPARATES STRONG LEADERS FROM WEAK ONES.
IF CONFLICTS AREN'T RESOLVED THROUGH POLITICS...
SOMEONE'S GONNA PULL OUT THE SPEARS.
AND THEN IT'S ALL OVER.
THUCYDIDES. SUCH A DRAMA QUEEN.

DEMOCRACY IS A PRETTY GOOD SYSTEM FOR MANAGING CONFLICT.
IN MY FAMILY, DEMOCRACY MOSTLY CREATES CONFLICT.
IN A DEMOCRATIC SOCIETY, WE KNOW WE'RE ALL IN THIS TOGETHER.
WHEN PEOPLE SEE THEY HAVE COMMON INTERESTS, THEY'RE LESS LIKELY TO RESORT TO VIOLENCE.

WE ALSO AVOID VIOLENCE BY PREVENTING THE WORST ABUSES OF POWER AND REWARDING GOOD LEADERSHIP.
WHO BETTER TO KEEP AN EYE ON THE LEADERS THAN THE CITIZENS?

SO, PEOPLE CAN DISAGREE ABOUT LEADERS, POLICIES, EVEN VALUES...
AS LONG AS THEY AGREE ON THE SYSTEM.

NO ONE EVEN *TRIED* TRAINING A BUNCH OF PHILOSOPHER-KINGS.
TWO THOUSAND FOUR HUNDRED YEARS AND HE'S STILL NOT OVER IT.

This is called a ***democratic consensus:*** principles about the function of government that all citizens share and uphold.

A democracy can only exist with the consent of the governed. It's like sitting down to play a game with friends: It only works if you all agree to play by the same rules.

DEMOCRATIC CONSENSUS IS THE SECRET SAUCE!
IS THE CONSTITUTION OUR DEMOCRATIC CONSENSUS?

Constitutions describe how societies plan to embody their democratic consensus, but they don't create it.

If society doesn't already embrace the deeper principles behind democracy, writing down "We the People" won't do much.

WHAT ARE THESE DEEPER PRINCIPLES?

1: All people are inherently equal.

THAT MEANS EQUAL IN PRACTICE, NOT JUST IN THE CONSTITUTION.

NO ONE'S RIGHTS ARE MORE SACRED THAN ANYONE ELSE'S.

AND OUR SAFETY, SECURITY, AND NEEDS ARE EQUALLY IMPORTANT.

2: Governments work better when lots of people are involved in decision-making.

NOBODY KNOWS EVERYTHING. WE CAN LEARN A LOT FROM OTHER PEOPLE.

EVEN PEOPLE WE DISAGREE WITH.

3: Competition for political power is a good thing.

AS LONG AS ALL COMPETITORS FOLLOW THE RULES.

I WAS HERE FIRST.

POLITICAL OPPOSITION IS PRETTY REVOLUTIONARY WHEN YOU THINK ABOUT IT.

NO, I WAS.

IF YOU CAN'T GET PEOPLE TO SUPPORT YOUR IDEAS WITH THEIR VOTE, WHY SHOULD YOU BE IN CHARGE?

4: Leaders should be accountable to their people.

I DON'T CARE IF YOUR TITLE IS MAYOR, SENATOR, OR PRESIDENT. YOU WORK FOR US.

IF YOU DON'T DELIVER OR YOU BREAK THE RULES...

WE'LL GIVE YOU THE BOOT.

Every democracy aspires to these principles—although few democracies live up to them all the time.

Democracies implement their principles through rights and procedures codified in law:
DIREC
CTORY
Elected officials
Free and fair elections
All citizens equal under the law
Access to information
Right to form associations, organizations, and political parties
Right to free expression
YUP, THOSE LOOK PRETTY FAMILIAR.
EXCUSE ME...
BUT ARE YOU WITH THOSE GUYS?
glasses galore
NO. WHY?
THEY'RE ARGUING ABOUT WHO IS VIRTUOUS ENOUGH FOR AVIATORS?
I CAN'T. I JUST CAN'T.
THEY WERE KIND OF HELPING US UNDERSTAND DEMOCRACY...
BUT THEY'RE REALLY HUNG UP ON FINDING A PERFECTLY VIRTUOUS LEADER.
ISN'T DEMOCRACY MOSTLY ABOUT GOVERNING WELL EVEN THOUGH NOBODY'S PERFECT?

SORRY TO INTERRUPT. I'M DAMONTE. NICE TO MEET Y'ALL.
KAMIAH, DID YOU FIND OUT ABOUT—
NO, THEY'RE NOT WITH THESE LADIES.
I GUESS SOMEONE'S HAVING A TOGA-THEMED THANKSGIVING?
DIRECTO
WE'RE TRYING TO FIGURE OUT WHAT MAKES A DEMOCRACY.

THERE'S THIS DEMOCRATIC CONSENSUS THING, BUT IS IT ENOUGH FOR EVERYONE TO AGREE ON PRINCIPLES?
HOW DO WE KNOW IF ENOUGH PEOPLE HAVE AGREED?

I'M NO EXPERT, BUT I DON'T THINK IT'S ONLY ABOUT A MAGIC NUMBER OF PEOPLE AGREEING ON PRINCIPLES.
WHAT ELSE DO YOU THINK WE NEED?

WELL, WHO'S A DEMOCRACY FOR?
AND WHO RUNS A DEMOCRACY?
THE PEOPLE WHO LIVE IN IT?
...ALSO THE PEOPLE?

IT DOESN'T MATTER HOW MANY PEOPLE SUPPORT DEMOCRACY IF THEY AREN'T ABLE TO PARTICIPATE IN IT.
IT'S NOT ENOUGH TO HAVE ELECTIONS AND SCRIBBLE DOWN SOME RIGHTS.

A REAL DEMOCRACY MAKES SURE PEOPLE HAVE THE CAPACITY TO BE ENGAGED CITIZENS.
WHAT DOES THAT TAKE?
I HOPE IT DOESN'T MEAN A TEST. I HATE TESTS.

SPEAKING FROM PERSONAL EXPERIENCE, ***FREE TIME*** TO GET INVOLVED IN THOSE ASSOCIATIONS WE HAVE THE RIGHT TO CREATE.

A ***GOOD EDUCATION*** SO WE CAN UNDERSTAND WHAT OUR CHOICES MIGHT MEAN.

MEASURES TO MAKE SURE OUR ***ECONOMIC STATUS*** DOESN'T LIMIT HOW MUCH WE CAN PARTICIPATE.

TRUST THAT OUR SKIN COLOR, GENDER, RELIGION, THE LANGUAGE WE SPEAK, OR WHATEVER WON'T KEEP US FROM OUR RIGHTS.

AREN'T THESE THINGS WE'RE SUPPOSED TO GET ***FROM*** DEMOCRACY?

For centuries, democrats have debated where to draw the line between the requirements and the rewards of democracy.
MINIMALIST
MAXIMALIST
DEMOCRACY SHOULD PROTECT CITIZENS FROM ARBITRARY RULERS AND GIVE THEM A ROLE IN DECISION-MAKING.
HOLD ON! YOU ALSO NEED POLITICAL AND SOCIOECONOMIC EQUALITY.
LIBERAL DEMOCRACY
SOCIAL DEMOCRACY
BUT DOESN'T EQUALITY COME FROM DEMOCRACY?
NOT AUTOMATICALLY.
DEMOCRACY GIVES US ALL THE *RIGHT* TO PARTICIPATE.
MY FRIEND OVER THERE THINKS RIGHTS ARE ALL YOU NEED.
BUT THERE'S A BIG GAP BETWEEN THE *RIGHT* AND THE *ABILITY*.
THOSE RIGHTS ARE THE TOOLS TO GET THE GOOD LIFE.
YOU CAN'T BLAME THE SYSTEM IF PEOPLE SIT ON THEIR THUMBS.
WE'RE NOT SITTING AROUND! WE'RE WORKING TWO JOBS, GOING BACK TO SCHOOL, RAISING KIDS—
IT'S A LOT EASIER FOR SOME PEOPLE TO GET INVOLVED THAN OTHERS.
LIKE THE RICH?
OR EDUCATED PEOPLE?

THE GOVERNMENT SHOULD BREAK DOWN THOSE BARRIERS.
YOU CAN'T HAVE A TRUE DEMOCRACY UNTIL PEOPLE HAVE EQUAL OPPORTUNITY IN PRACTICE *AND* ON PAPER.
BUT WHAT DOES THAT ACTUALLY LOOK LIKE?

REGULATIONS TO KEEP MONEY AND POWER FROM CONSTANTLY FLOWING UPWARD.
EASY ACCESS TO BASIC NEEDS LIKE EDUCATION, HEALTH CARE, AND HOUSING.
WAYS TO PARTICIPATE EVEN IF YOU CAN'T AFFORD YOUR OWN LOBBYIST.

MY UNCLE AND HIS FRIENDS MAKE SOCIALIST DEMOCRACY SOUND REALLY DANGEROUS.
LIKE, THE GOVERNMENT WILL TAKE THINGS AWAY FROM US.

IT'S NOT ABOUT TAKING AWAY.
IT'S ABOUT MAKING SURE ALL PEOPLE HAVE THE RESOURCES AND OPPORTUNITIES TO BE FULLY ACTIVE CITIZENS.
BUT THAT'S SO OBVIOUS! I CAN'T BELIEVE MY FAMILY FIGHTS ABOUT THAT EVERY TIME WE GET TOGETHER!

BUT YOU SAID YOU BELIEVE IN EQUALITY, TOO.
NATURALLY. ***POLITICAL EQUALITY*** IS CENTRAL TO ANY DEMOCRATIC SYSTEM.
BUT DEMOCRACY ISN'T BROKEN JUST BECAUSE THERE ISN'T SOCIAL OR ECONOMIC EQUALITY.
EVEN IF IT MEANS NOT EVERYONE CAN PARTICIPATE EQUALLY?

BUT THEY CAN, AS LONG AS THEY CAN ALL VOTE.
THEY CAN ELECT WORKING-CLASS REPRESENTATIVES. THEY CAN VOTE FOR UNIVERSAL HEALTH CARE.

VOTING IS WHAT MAKES A TRUE DEMOCRACY.
I SEE.

YOUR IDEA OF EQUAL PARTICIPATION IS HERE–

–AND YOUR IDEA IS WAY UP HERE.

IS THERE SUCH A THING AS THE RIGHT AMOUNT OF PARTICIPATION?
THE JURY'S STILL OUT.

History is full of experiments in participatory government.

For example, towns and cities gathering to solve problems together.

ALL IN FAVOR OF INCREASING THE WOOL TAX, RAISE YOUR HANDS.

CITIZENS ASSEMBLY IN ATHENS, FIFTH CENTURY BCE

DEMOCRATIC REPUBLIC OF GRAUBUNDEN, SIXTEENTH CENTURY

VIKING TING, TENTH CENTURY

Or monarchs consulting with their subjects...

SIGNING OF THE MAGNA CARTA, ENGLAND, 1215

We've tested democratic innovations in brand-new nations.

UNITY IN BOTSWANA WILL NOT BE ACHIEVED BY LEGISLATION, BUT BY CONSULTATION AND CONSENSUS.

SERETSE KHAMA, FIRST PRESIDENT OF BOTSWANA, 1971

AND WITH THAT, INDIA BECOMES THE WORLD'S LARGEST DEMOCRACY!

MUMBAI, 1947

And built on a long tradition of consultation and cooperation.
HAUDENOSAUNEE CONFEDERACY MEETING IN COUNCIL
PRE-CONTACT
TODAY
Using constitutions, written and unwritten.
UTTARAMERUR CONSTITUTION (MODERN-DAY TAMIL NADU) FOR VILLAGE-LEVEL DEMOCRACY, TENTH CENTURY
CARRIE CHAPMAN CATT, U.S. SUFFRAGIST AND POLITICAL ORGANIZER
I PROCLAIM THE KOUROUKAN FOUGA, OUR CHARTER OF RIGHTS AND GOVERNMENT…
SUNDIATA KEITA, FOUNDER OF THE MALI EMPIRE, THIRTEENTH CENTURY

Democracy means experimenting with who sits at the table.
ARE REPRESENTATIVES FROM ALL THE CLANS HERE?
VAINAKH PEOPLE'S COUNCIL, MODERN-DAY CHECHNYA, FIFTEENTH CENTURY
WOMEN WANT THE VOTE
Let us vote
NEW ZEALAND, 1893
It means demanding that the people have a say, over and over again.
YELLOW REVOLUTION PHILIPPINES 1986
ROSE REVOLUTION
GEORGIA 2003
THE COLOR REVOLUTIONS, 1986–2007
VELVET REVOLUTION
CZECHOSLOVAKIA
1989
BURMA
SAFFRON REVOLUTION 2007

It means pushing forward even if the government tries to shut you up...
CHILE, 1974
...even if you're not sure anyone can hear you.
UMBRELLA MOVEMENT FOR DEMOCRACY, HONG KONG, 2014
TIANANMEN SQUARE, CHINA, 1989
Because democracy promises what no other government will guarantee.
ARAB SPRING, 2010
REEDOM
RESPECT THE WILL OF THE PEOPLE
HUMAN RIGHTS
DIGNITY
LISTEN
US

There's no one right way to participate in government.
Every democracy develops its own unique ecosystem, but they grow from the same seeds.
WOW. IT FEELS KIND OF EPIC TO FIGHT FOR DEMOCRACY.
FORTUNATELY, MOST OF THE TIME YOU DON'T HAVE TO ACTUALLY FIGHT.
DEMOCRACY'S BEST DEFENDERS ARE PEOPLE WHO GET INVOLVED IN THE NITTY-GRITTY DAILY WORK.
SO HOW DO WE FIND THE RIGHT WAY FOR ***OUR*** DEMOCRACY?
TO ANSWER THAT QUESTION, WE HAVE TO ASK A FEW OTHERS.
WHO is participating?
HOW do they participate?
WHAT do citizens need to participate meaningfully?

I THOUGHT EVERYONE WAS SUPPOSED TO PARTICIPATE.

IN AN IDEAL DEMOCRACY, EVERY *ADULT CITIZEN* PARTICIPATES IN VARIOUS WAYS. LIKE VOTING.

OR HOLDING OFFICE.

OR ADDING YOUR PIECE TO THE POLITICAL AGENDA.

BUT WE DON'T LIVE IN AN IDEAL DEMOCRACY, DO WE?

ASK YOURSELVES, WHO COUNTS AS A CITIZEN?

WELL, ISN'T *EVERYBODY* A CITIZEN?

BOY, IS *THAT* A LOADED QUESTION.

The concept of citizenship has changed quite a bit over time. The first Athenian democracy had five types of citizenship, based on wealth and status.

PENTA-COSIO-MEDIMNI
Eligible to become archons (rulers).
AREOPAGUS
Former archons. Serve as judges.
HIPPEIS
Eligible to join Council of 400, hold senior government posts, join the cavalry.
GRAIN
ZEUGITAE
Eligible to join Council of 400, hold minor government posts, join the infantry.
THETES
Eligible to sit in the Citizen's Assembly, row war galleys.
NOT CITIZENS
No rights, no voice, no role.

In the Roman Republic, geography dictated your status.
CITIZENS
NOT CITIZENS

Citizenship was a hot-button issue.
THE ITALIANS ARE THE BACKBONE OF OUR ECONOMY AND THE SOLDIERS IN OUR WORLD-FAMOUS ARMY.
IT'S PAST TIME WE MADE THEM CITIZENS!
BUT THERE ARE SO MANY OF THEM!
WHAT IF THEY OUT-VOTE *REAL* ROMANS?

Citizenship has been an important and controversial issue ever since, especially in the United States.
RULERS ONLY.
FEUDAL LORDS!
AND RELIGIOUS LEADERS!
LANDOWNERS!
MERCHANTS AND TAXPAYERS!
MEN!
WEALTHY MEN!
WHITE MEN.
FINE, WHITE *PEOPLE*.
EVERY SINGLE ADULT.
Tenth century
1960s

The Framers of the U.S. Constitution made rules about who could be a citizen and what that meant.
IN OUR NEW COUNTRY, ANY CITIZEN WHO OWNS LAND CAN VOTE!
ANY *MALE* CITIZEN, YOU MEAN.
RIGHT, OBVIOUSLY.

Then they changed their minds.
SORRY, WE MEANT ONLY FREE WHITE LAND-OWNING MALES.

Again.
IT SEEMS LIKE ANYBODY CAN BE A LANDOWNER THESE DAYS.
WHAT IF WE SAID YOU HAD TO OWN *ENOUGH* LAND?

And again.
WELCOME TO AMERICA!
A PASSPORT FOR YOU, AND ONE FOR YOU, AND...
YOU CAN ONLY VOTE IF YOU SPEAK ENGLISH.

And again.
IF WE WANT ALL THOSE BIG CITY BUSINESSMEN TO KEEP PAYING TAXES, WE'RE GOING TO HAVE TO GIVE THEM A SAY.
RALEIGH
GOOD NEWS, IF YOU'RE A TAX-PAYING MALE CITIZEN, YOU'RE NOW A VOTER, TOO!

But...
NOT YOU.
POLL

BUT THE FIFTEENTH AMENDMENT SAYS—
NEVER HEARD OF IT.

No one but white men got to participate without a struggle.
1872
VOTES FOR WOMEN
VOTES FOR WOMEN
VOTES FOR WOMEN
WHITE WOMEN DIDN'T GET THE VOTE UNTIL 1919. OTHER WOMEN HAD TO WAIT EVEN LONGER.
IN THE CASE OF ***ELK V. WILKINS,*** WE FIND THAT NATIVE AMERICANS ARE NOT CITIZENS AND CANNOT VOTE.
1884

1882
San Francisco Chronicle
EXCLUSION ACT SAYS NO CITIZENSHIP OR VOTE FOR CHINESE
MY IN-LAWS KNOW ALL ABOUT THAT ONE.

NATIVE AMERICANS WEREN'T LEGALLY RECOGNIZED AS CITIZENS UNTIL 1924.
1952 FOR ASIAN AMERICANS.
AND ALL OF THAT HAPPENS BEFORE WE EVEN GET TO THE CIVIL RIGHTS MOVEMENT.
GOSH. I THOUGHT IT WAS LIKE ***BOOM,*** END OF SLAVERY, ***BOOM,*** NINETEENTH AMENDMENT, ***BOOM,*** CIVIL RIGHTS.

IT'S TAKEN TWO CENTURIES TO PRY THE DOORS OPEN WIDE ENOUGH FOR EVERY ADULT CITIZEN TO WALK THROUGH.

ALL THAT JUST TO MARK YOUR BALLOT, WHICH IS A TINY PART OF HAVING AN EQUAL SAY.

DEMOCRACIES NEED THEIR CITIZENS TO DO MORE THAN FILL IN A BUBBLE.

EXCUSE ME.

DID YOU NEED SOMETHING, HONEY?
IT'S GREAT THAT ALL YOU ADULTS GET A SAY, BUT WHAT ABOUT KIDS?
WE'RE ALREADY DOING THE WORK...
AND DEALING WITH THE CONSEQUENCES...
LONG BEFORE WE'RE ELIGIBLE TO VOTE.
PROTECT KIDS NOT GUNS
FEAR HAS NO PLACE IN SCHOOLS
MARCH FOR OUR LIVES !!!
IN MEMORY
SANDY HOOK
Democracy means working to include everyone with a stake in the decisions our leaders make.
When we ask who participates, we have to keep in mind everybody who belongs at the table.
RESTAURANT DIRECTORY
IF WHO PARTICIPATES IS ABOUT MAKING SURE EVERYONE IS AT THE TABLE...
HOW THEY PARTICIPATE IS LIKE HAVING MANY DIFFERENT TABLES TO SIT AT.

A REPRESENTATIVE TASTE
PRESIDENTIAL BURGER
THE PARLIAMENTARY CAFE
ALL YOU CAN VOTE

WHAT ARE THEY SERVING?
THE DIFFERENT FLAVORS OF DEMOCRACY.

DEMOCRACY HAS FLAVORS, TOO?
DEMOCRACIES HAVE LOTS OF DIFFERENT SYSTEMS FOR CITIZEN PARTICIPATION.

a Representative Taste
IN A *REPRESENTATIVE DEMOCRACY*...
CITIZENS CHOOSE PEOPLE TO SERVE AS THEIR CHAMPIONS IN THE DECISION-MAKING PROCESS.

I KNOW THIS ONE!
IT'S WHERE WE PICK PEOPLE TO ACT FOR US AND HANDLE THE EVERYDAY GOVERNMENT STUFF.
I THOUGHT THAT WAS JUST HOW DEMOCRACY WORKED.
THAT IS A VERY POPULAR OPTION.
BUT WE HAVE A NUMBER OF REPRESENTATIVE PROFILES FOR YOU TO CHOOSE FROM.
FOR INSTANCE, BY POPULATION SIZE.
Endorsed by the U.S. House of Representatives!
OR BY TERRITORY.
A senatorial favorite!
PERHAPS BY RELIGIOUS OR ETHNIC IDENTITY?
Consociational cuisine!
TRIBE OR CLAN, FOR THOSE WITH TRADITIONAL PREFERENCES.
A taste of home!
AND IF YOU'RE A RISK TAKER, ALLOW ME TO RECOMMEND THE LOTTERY.
Chef's choice!

WHAT IF YOU DON'T WANT REPRESENTATIVES?

ALL YOU CAN VOTE!
THEN YOU MAY WISH TO VISIT ONE OF OUR COMPETITORS.

In a ***direct democracy,*** the citizens make most decisions without any intermediary.
EVERY CITIZEN CAN PARTICIPATE IN EVERY DECISION.
THAT SOUNDS EXHAUSTING.
AND TIME-CONSUMING.

IT WORKS WELL FOR SMALL COMMUNITIES, LIKE TOWNS OR VILLAGES.
WE HAVE DIRECT DEMOCRACY RIGHT HERE IN AMERICA, YOU KNOW.
ALL YOU CAN VOTE!
WE DO?

OF COURSE! WE HAVE THOSE IN CALIFORNIA.
TRY
INITIATIVE AND REFERENDUM

An ***initiative*** is when the people draft a law and vote on it directly, without going through the legislature.

INITIATIVE

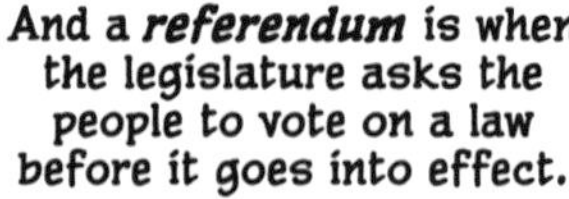
And a ***referendum*** is when the legislature asks the people to vote on a law before it goes into effect.

REFERENDUM

I NEVER KNEW YOU COULD DO THAT IN AMERICA!
SOMETIMES IT'S GREAT. IF THE LEGISLATURE WON'T DEAL WITH SOMETHING, WE CAN HANDLE IT OURSELVES.

BUT IT'S NOT ALWAYS EASY. SOME YEARS THERE ARE DOZENS OF MEASURES TO VOTE ON.

SOME TOPICS ARE REALLY COMPLEX. IT'S HARD TO UNDERSTAND WHAT A "YES" OR "NO" VOTE MEANS.
HMM, YEAH.
I LIKE IT WHEN OUR REPRESENTATIVES DO THE TRICKY DECISION-MAKING.
I'M NOT SURE A WHOLE COUNTRY COULD RUN BY REFERENDUM.

THIS IS ACTUALLY HOW WE DO THINGS IN SWITZERLAND, MY COUNTRY.
NO WAY! HOW DOES IT WORK?

WE HAVE THREE LEVELS OF GOVERNMENT: COMMUNAL, CANTONAL, AND FEDERAL.
EACH LEVEL MAKES DECISIONS FOR ITS OWN TERRITORY.

WE STILL HAVE A PARLIAMENT WITH LIMITED POWER TO MAKE OR CHANGE LAWS.
BUT THE PEOPLE CAN MAKE LAWS, TOO, THROUGH THE POPULAR INITIATIVE.
LIKE HERE.

SWISS CITIZENS MUST BE VERY INFORMED ALL THE TIME.
CITIZENS *SHOULD* KNOW WHAT THEIR GOVERNMENT IS DOING, BUT THAT SOUNDS LIKE A LOT OF WORK.

HOW DO YOU KEEP FROM HAVING GIANT NATIONAL FIGHTS ALL THE TIME?
HUNDREDS OF YEARS OF PRACTICE! WE HAD TO LEARN HOW TO DISAGREE BUT KEEP TALKING.
IT HELPS THAT WE ARE A SMALL NATION OF PEOPLE WITH SIMILAR BACKGROUNDS.

JUST LIKE THAT PHILOSOPHER SAID: THE GOAL IS USEFUL CONFLICT WITHOUT VIOLENCE.

SO WE HAVE REPRESENTATIVE DEMOCRACY AND DIRECT DEMOCRACY.
ARE THERE MORE KINDS?

SOMETIMES WE DECIDE HOW PEOPLE SHOULD PARTICIPATE BASED ON WHAT KIND OF DECISIONS NEED TO BE MADE.
SAY WHAT?

Citizens can play an important role, even if they aren't the final decision-makers. In *participatory democracy,* the goal is to get as many people participating as possible.
TRY OUR SALSAS!
VOTE ON YOUR FAVORITE
MILD
MEDIUM
SPICY
HOT!
LIKE INITIATIVES AND REFERENDUMS.
OR TOWN HALLS.
OR POLITICAL OPINION SURVEYS.

SOMETIMES IT'S GOOD TO KNOW WHAT A LOT OF PEOPLE THINK ABOUT A QUESTION.
IT HELPS THE DECISION-MAKERS NARROW THEIR OPTIONS.
WHAT IF THE QUESTION IS REALLY COMPLICATED? NOT EVERYTHING CAN BE SOLVED WITH A SURVEY.

Deliberative democracy is useful when there's a lot of information to go through or when the decision affects some people more than the general population.
SAY yum TO THE CAKE!

I THINK WE'D BETTER TASTE THEM ALL.
CAN WE INTERVIEW THE BAKERS?
WHERE DO YOU GET YOUR FLOUR FROM?

I'VE SEEN THIS IN ACTION!
OUR STAKEHOLDER COMMITTEES REPRESENT ALL THE GROUPS WHO USE OUR WATER RESOURCES.
THEY MAKE RECOMMENDATIONS TO THE BOARD OF DIRECTORS.
THE BOARD MAKES THE FINAL DECISION, BUT THESE GROUPS HELP US UNDERSTAND WHAT IS MOST IMPORTANT TO THEIR COMMUNITIES.

SO IT'S LIKE HAVING EXPERTS...
BUT THE THING THEY'RE EXPERTS IN IS THEIR NEIGHBORHOOD?

THEY'RE EXPERTS IN HOW A PARTICULAR WATERSHED IS USED.
THEY KNOW THINGS YOU ONLY LEARN FROM BEING PART OF THE LIFE THERE.

TALKING TO THE PEOPLE AFFECTED IS ALWAYS A GOOD IDEA. YOU NEVER KNOW WHAT ISSUES YOU'VE OVERLOOKED.
THEY MIGHT EVEN HAVE SOLUTIONS YOU NEVER THOUGHT OF.

COUNTRIES CAN PICK THE SYSTEM THAT WORKS BEST FOR THEM OR EVEN USE MORE THAN ONE.
THAT'S KIND OF COOL.

BUT HOW DO YOU KNOW WHICH TO USE WHEN?
IS THAT WHAT THE CONSTITUTION IS FOR?
SOMETIMES.
BUT CONSTITUTIONS DON'T TELL US HOW TO HANDLE EVERY SITUATION.
SOMETIMES WE HAVE TO EXPERIMENT AND SEE WHAT WORKS.

The trick is to stop thinking of democracy as a one-way street.

THE PEOPLE ELECT REPRESENTATIVES

REPRESENTATIVES MAKE LAWS

THE GOVERNMENT ENFORCES THE LAWS

THAT ISN'T HOW IT WORKS?
DEMOCRACY IS ALL ABOUT MORE PEOPLE MAKING BETTER DECISIONS TOGETHER.
IT'S NOT JUST CASTING A BALLOT AND WALKING AWAY.

I CAN SHOW YOU. HOLD ON...

MIND IF I BORROW THIS?
ROLL

WHAT? NO! THAT'S MINE!
IT'S FOR A GOOD CAUSE!

IN A REPRESENTATIVE DEMOCRACY LIKE OURS, CITIZENS VOTE.
BUT...
THEY CAN ALSO RUN FOR OFFICE!
WHAT'S THIS?
THAT'S MY—
SHOVE!
CANDIDATES WIN VOTES BY PROMISING TO DO CERTAIN THINGS.
BUT THEY DON'T COME UP WITH ALL THOSE IDEAS BY THEMSELVES!
YOU CARRY THE SUITCASE OF IDEAS...
...BUT YOUR FELLOW CITIZENS HELP TO FILL IT UP.

CITIZEN INTEREST GROUPS ALSO ASK CANDIDATES TO CARRY CERTAIN ISSUES.
FREE PRE-K

YOU DON'T EVEN HAVE TO WAIT FOR A CANDIDATE TO LISTEN TO YOU.
TAKE YOUR ISSUE PUBLIC, SEE IF OTHER PEOPLE AGREE.
THEN THE CANDIDATES OR OTHER ELECTED OFFICIALS WILL GET INTERESTED, TOO.

WHAT IF I DON'T LIKE WHAT SHE'S CARRYING?
OR SHE DOESN'T LISTEN TO ME?

NO PROBLEM!

YOU CAN RUN, TOO!

OR YOU CAN VOTE FOR SOMEONE ELSE.

ELECTION VOLUNTEER
VOTE!
YOU CAN EVEN PARTICIPATE WITHOUT CHOOSING A SIDE.

OKAY, THERE ARE LOTS OF WAYS TO GET INVOLVED DURING AN ELECTION.
BUT DON'T OUR REPRESENTATIVES HANDLE THINGS AFTER THAT?
ISN'T THAT WHY WE ***HAVE*** REPRESENTATIVES?

NO WAY! THEY MANAGE THE DAY-TO-DAY STUFF...
BUT DEMOCRACIES DON'T WORK IF PEOPLE ONLY SHOW UP DURING ELECTIONS.

YOU'VE MADE ALL THESE PROMISES. BUT HOW WILL YOU DECIDE WHAT TO UNPACK FIRST?
DON'T YOU DARE UNPACK ANYTHING!

I'M GONNA GUESS YOU ASK THE PEOPLE.
DO "THE PEOPLE" ALWAYS KNOW THE RIGHT ANSWER?

I KNOW TOO MANY PEOPLE WHO DON'T PAY ATTENTION...
OR ONLY PAY ATTENTION TO WHAT AFFECTS THEM DIRECTLY.

"MY FAMILY HAS THIS HOBBY.

"BUT THEN ONE DAY, THEY CHANGED THE RULES.

EAGLE ROCK ATV PARK

No children under the age of 13 allowed to ride

"I GET THIS ISN'T THE BIGGEST PROBLEM IN THE WORLD.

"BUT IT'S OUR FAMILY'S THING."

"WE WERE PRETTY MAD ABOUT IT.
WHY DO THEY WANNA MAKE IT SO WE CAN'T HAVE FUN WITH OUR KIDS?
THESE BIG CITY POLITICIANS JUST DON'T GET IT.
IT'S THE NANNY STATE, YOU KNOW?

WE OUGHTA DO SOMETHING!

SAFETY FIRST
LET OUR KIDS PLAY
SAFE FOR ALL
TRUST OUR KIDS
SAFETY FIRST
"AT FIRST, I DIDN'T HAVE A LOT OF RESPECT FOR THE OTHER SIDE.
KEEP OUR KIDS SAFE
HAVE YOU EVER BEEN ON AN ATV? OUR KIDS AREN'T THE PROBLEM!

"WE DIDN'T EXPECT POLITICIANS TO CARE WHAT WE THOUGHT. BUT ONE OF THE LEGISLATORS FROM THE OTHER SIDE LISTENED TO US. HE HELPED US TALK TO EACH OTHER."

THIS IS BIGGER THAN SOME FAMILY FUN.
YOUR BILL WOULD KEEP KIDS FROM USING ATVS TO HELP OUT ON FAMILY FARMS.

BUT AN ATV WILL CRUSH A SMALL PERSON IF IT FLIPS OVER, NO MATTER HOW GOOD A RIDER THEY ARE.
I NEVER THOUGHT OF THAT.
I NEVER THOUGHT OF ***THAT.***

"IN THE END, WE CAME UP WITH A COMPROMISE.
KEEP KIDS AFE!
"RIDERS UNDER TWELVE NOW HAVE TO TAKE A TRAINING COURSE, WEAR A HELMET, AND RIDE SMALLER ATVS...
"BUT EVERYBODY CAN KEEP RIDING TOGETHER."

IT WAS KIND OF A GAME-CHANGER.
I THOUGHT THE GOVERNMENT JUST MADE THINGS HARDER FOR PEOPLE LIKE ME.
BUT THEY LISTENED, EVEN WHEN THEY DISAGREED WITH US.
WE DIDN'T GET EVERYTHING WE WANTED, BUT IT ENDED UP OKAY.

DEMOCRACY DOESN'T MEAN EVERYONE GETS THEIR FIRST CHOICE.
HE'S RIGHT! IT MEANS WE KEEP TALKING UNTIL EVERYONE SAYS, "YEAH, I CAN LIVE WITH THAT."
THAT STORY WOULD HAVE HAD A BAD ENDING WITHOUT "THE PEOPLE" GETTING INVOLVED.

ELECTED REPRESENTATIVES AREN'T PERFECT AND ALL-KNOWING. THEY NEED OUR HELP TO FIND THE MIDDLE GROUND.

EVEN SO, WE DON'T ALWAYS GET IT RIGHT THE FIRST TIME.
OUR FIRST SOLUTION MIGHT NOT WORK FOR EVERYBODY.

OR IT MIGHT BE MISSING SOMETHING IMPORTANT.
WHERE ARE THE BOTTOMS?

BUT REPRESENTATIVES WILL NEVER KNOW THAT UNLESS CITIZENS TELL THEM.
I'M TELLING *YOU* THAT MY SWIMSUIT IS NOT UP FOR DEBATE!
SWIPE!

OUR CITY HALL PUT IN A NEW "ACCESSIBLE" ENTRANCE BACK IN THE EARLY '90S.
BOY, IS *THAT* EVER TRUE!
BUT THERE WAS A PROBLEM WITH THE RAMP.
IT WAS TOO STEEP?
THEY NEVER ASKED FOR INPUT FROM THOSE OF US WHO WOULD ACTUALLY HAVE TO USE IT.
THAT'S DOING DEMOCRACY BACKWARD.
FOR SURE.
MY FRIEND AND I DECIDED TO MAKE A LITTLE FUSS.
WE DIDN'T EXPECT ANYTHING TO COME OF IT, BUT...
DANGER STEEP
DANGER

CHANNEL 6
Evening News
MAYBE SKATERS WILL USE IT, BUT I CAN'T.
CITY HALL RENOVATIONS FALL SHORT

MAKE CITY HALL TRULY ACCESSIBLE!
SIGN THE PETITION

MEN WORKING

OUR CITY COUNCIL HAD TO LEARN A LOT FROM ME, BUT THEY PUT IN THE WORK.
AND THEN THEY ASKED ME TO HELP THEM WRITE ACCESSIBILITY GUIDELINES FOR ALL PUBLIC CITY BUILDINGS!
I'M THINKING THAT COULD ONLY HAPPEN IN A DEMOCRACY.

DEMOCRACY GAVE LITTLE OL' ME THE RIGHT TO DEMAND THEY FIX THE PROBLEM.

SPEAKING OF RIGHTS, WE USED A LOT OF THEM!

THE RIGHT TO EXPRESS AN OPINION, TALKING TO THE FREE PRESS, FORMING AN ORGANIZATION TO ADVOCATE, SUBMITTING A PETITION—

THE RIGHT TO DRAW ON GOVERNMENT PROPERTY?
A LITTLE SIDEWALK CHALK NEVER HURT NOBODY.

THE CITY COUNCIL'S RESPONSE WAS PRETTY DEMOCRATIC, TOO.
LISTENING TO YOU, FIXING THE PROBLEM, THEN INVITING YOU TO HELP MAKE IT SO IT WOULDN'T HAPPEN AGAIN.
THEY DIDN'T WANT THE BAD PUBLICITY.
BUT HEY, THAT'S ALSO DEMOCRATIC: BAD PUBLICITY MEANS YOU MIGHT LOSE AN ELECTION.
THANKS FOR VOTING!
PAY HERE

THERE'S SOMETHING ABOUT BOTH YOUR STORIES.
YOU FELT LIKE THE GOVERNMENT LET YOU DOWN, BUT YOU DIDN'T LOSE FAITH IN DEMOCRACY.

UH...NO? I WAS MAD THEY SCREWED UP, BUT THE GOVERNMENT IS BIGGER THAN MY ONE PROBLEM.
AND I JUST FIGURED WE NEEDED DIFFERENT PEOPLE IN OFFICE.

LEGITIMACY!

THEY DIDN'T FEEL LIKE THEY HAD TO CHANGE THE WHOLE SYSTEM, EVEN THOUGH THEY FELT IGNORED OR EXCLUDED.
THAT'S BECAUSE THERE WAS A BUILT-IN WAY TO MAKE CHANGES.

THAT'S PRETTY DIFFERENT FROM THOSE OTHER GOVERNMENTS WE SAW.

IT FEELS MORE... FLEXIBLE, YOU KNOW?
AND RESILIENT!

THEY DIDN'T EVEN HAVE TO WAIT FOR AN ELECTION WHEN THEY SAW SOMETHING GOING WRONG.
EXIT
EXIT
IN A DEMOCRACY, CITIZENS CAN GET STARTED ON FIXING PROBLEMS RIGHT AWAY.

ELECTIONS ARE MORE LIKE A CHECK-IN, NOT OUR ONE BIG SHOT.
I NEVER UNDERSTOOD THAT DEMOCRACY GAVE US SO MANY WAYS TO GET TO A BETTER OUTCOME.

YOU CAN VOTE FOR PEOPLE WHOSE IDEAS YOU LIKE.
YOU CAN ADD YOUR PRIORITIES TO THE POLITICAL AGENDA.
YOU DON'T HAVE TO DO IT ALONE OR WAIT FOR SOME ELECTED OFFICIAL TO CARE. YOU CAN FIND OR ORGANIZE A GROUP TO WORK ON IT TOGETHER.
AND THAT'S ALL PART OF A DEMOCRATIC SYSTEM WORKING THE WAY IT'S SUPPOSED TO.
YOU CAN PROPOSE YOUR OWN IDEAS.
THERE ARE TONS OF WAYS TO CHANGE BILLS BEFORE THEY TURN INTO LAWS, AND EVEN AFTER.
THE ONLY ABSOLUTELY ESSENTIAL THING IS...WELL, US, I GUESS...
ALL YOU CAN VOTE!

TO GATES
DEMOCRACIES DON'T ALWAYS WORK LIKE THEY'RE SUPPOSED TO, OF COURSE.
SOMETIMES THEY'RE DESIGNED TO FAIL.
THAT'S WHY IT'S SO IMPORTANT THAT WE DO OUR PART:
STAY ENGAGED, HOLD OUR LEADERS ACCOUNTABLE, RAISE OUR KIDS TO BE ACTIVE CITIZENS.
GEEZ, SO IT SEEMS LIKE WE NEED TO KNOW A LOT TO DO OUR JOB AS CITIZENS.
WHAT'S GOING ON?
WHAT'S THE HISTORY?
WHAT'S THE ACTUAL PROBLEM WE'RE TRYING TO SOLVE?
WHO'S INVOLVED?
WHO HASN'T BEEN INVOLVED BUT SHOULD BE?
WHAT ARE THE CONSEQUENCES OF DIFFERENT CHOICES?
SOME ISSUES ARE SO COMPLICATED WE NEED PEOPLE WHO CAN HELP US UNDERSTAND.
PEOPLE WHO KNOW THE COMMUNITY INVOLVED, OR WHO ARE EXPERTS IN THE SUBJECT.
THE OTHER THING WE NEED IS ACCESS TO INFORMATION.
RIGHT. THE FREE PRESS, MEDIA WE CAN TRUST.

THAT'S PART OF IT, BUT I'M THINKING BIGGER THAN THAT.
ACCESS TO INFORMATION IS A FUNDAMENTAL HUMAN RIGHT.
Article 19
Universal Declaration of Human Rights
Everyone has the right to freedom of opinion and expression; this right includes freedom to hold opinions without interference and to seek, receive, and impart information and ideas through any media and regardless of frontiers.
THAT *IS* A LOT BIGGER.
NO ONE'S AN EXPERT ON EVERY ISSUE.
SO IF WE WANT PEOPLE TO GET INVOLVED, THEY GOTTA BE ABLE TO LEARN ABOUT STUFF.

WE ALSO NEED INFORMATION TO KNOW IF OUR GOVERNMENT IS KEEPING ITS PROMISES.
DEMOCRATIC SOCIETIES AROUND THE WORLD AGREE THAT INFORMED CITIZENS MAKE GOVERNMENT WORK BETTER.

DEMOCRACY CAN'T FUNCTION UNLESS WE CAN GET THE INFORMATION WE NEED WHEN WE NEED IT.
WHICH IS WHY WE'VE PASSED LAWS TO GUARANTEE ACCESS TO ALL KINDS OF INFORMATION.

Freedom of Information Act

§ 552. Public information; agency rules, opinions, orders, records, and proceedings

Each agency shall make available to the public information as follows:

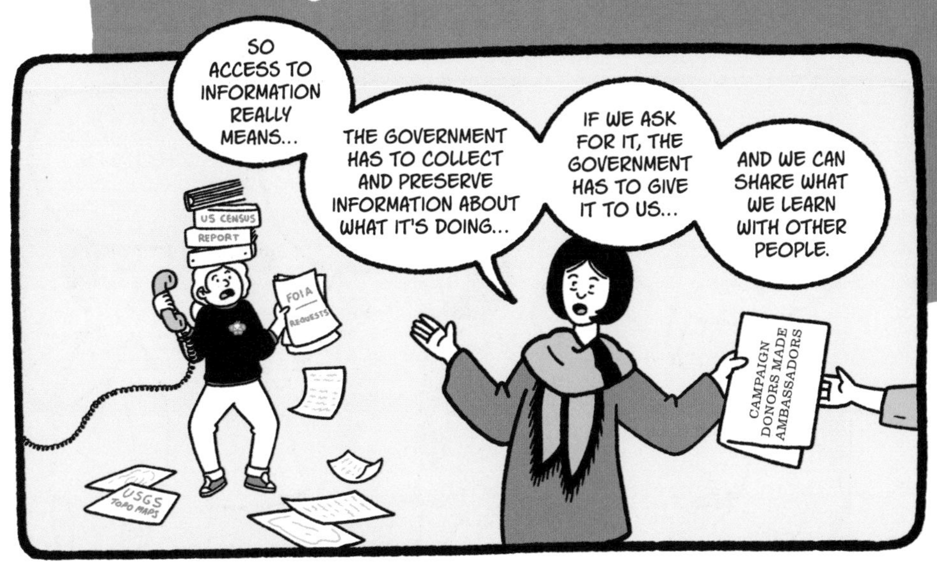

SO ACCESS TO INFORMATION REALLY MEANS...
THE GOVERNMENT HAS TO COLLECT AND PRESERVE INFORMATION ABOUT WHAT IT'S DOING...
IF WE ASK FOR IT, THE GOVERNMENT HAS TO GIVE IT TO US...
AND WE CAN SHARE WHAT WE LEARN WITH OTHER PEOPLE.
US CENSUS
REPORT
FOIA REQUESTS
USGS TOPO MAPS
CAMPAIGN DONORS MADE AMBASSADORS

AND THE GOVERNMENT CAN'T INTERFERE WITH ANY OF THAT, RIGHT?
NOT IN A HEALTHY DEMOCRACY.

THERE ARE SOME EXCEPTIONS FOR NATIONAL SECURITY AND PROTECTING PRIVACY...
BUT THE GOVERNMENT SHOULDN'T PUT UP BARRIERS, INCLUDING MAKING IT EXPENSIVE OR TIME-CONSUMING TO ACCESS INFORMATION.

WHEN THE FOLKS IN CHARGE START TRYING TO HIDE THE DATA, WE SHOULD ALL GET WORRIED.
AND MAD.

OF COURSE, YOU CAN HAVE ALL THE INFORMATION IN THE WORLD SITTING RIGHT AT YOUR FEET...
BUT IT DOES YOU NO GOOD IF YOU DON'T KNOW WHERE TO GET IT AND HOW TO USE IT.
THAT'S WHY WE NEED GOOD SCHOOLS AS WELL AS ACCESS TO INFORMATION.

Freedom of information helps us make sure they're working as they should.

APPRO-PRIATIONS

Education gives us the tools to get information, understand it, and keep government accountable.

HM, YOU MEAN LIKE—

I SEE.

SORRY, I COULDN'T HELP BUT OVERHEAR.
BUT WE CAN'T PUT ALL THE BURDEN ON CITIZENS.
WE HAVE TO ENGAGE, BUT DEMOCRACY IS A CONVERSATION. OUR LEADERS ALSO HAVE TO LISTEN.
WE CAN'T DO OUR JOB AS CITIZENS IF THE PEOPLE IN CHARGE AREN'T MAKING SPACE FOR US.
YOU'RE RIGHT!
WE HAVE STRUGGLED WITH THIS IN ECUADOR FOR DECADES.
WE LIKE TO THINK OF A DEMOCRACY AS A NATION FULL OF PEOPLE WITH THE SAME GOALS AND IDEAS.
BUT THAT'S NOT ALWAYS THE CASE.
WE HAVE FIVE HUNDRED YEARS OF COLONIAL LEGACY. THAT HISTORY CASTS ITS SHADOW OVER EVERYTHING.
LIMIT MINING
honor our PEOPLES
LIMIT OIL EXTRACTION
EQUAL
LAND THEFT
OUR INDIGENOUS NATIONS EXISTED FOR THOUSANDS OF YEARS BEFORE ECUADOR, BUT MOST ECUADOREANS TREAT US LIKE A SILENT PEOPLE.
WE DEMAND EQUAL ACCESS TO WATER
WE STRUGGLED FOR DECADES TO REGAIN OUR VOICES.

IN 1998, WE FINALLY WON A NEW CONSTITUTION...
WHICH RECOGNIZED ECUADOR AS A *PLURINATIONAL DEMOCRACY:*
MANY NATIONS, EACH WITH THEIR OWN CULTURE, LANGUAGE, TERRITORY, AND VISION OF A GOOD FUTURE.
TSÁCHILA
CHACHI
EPERA
AWÃ
SHUAR
ACHUAR
QUECHUA
SHIWIAR
COFÁN
SIONA
SECOYA
ZÁPARA
ANDOA Y WAORANI
THE COUNTRY CAN ONLY THRIVE BY BALANCING THE INTERESTS OF ALL ITS NATIONS AND INCLUDING THEM IN CRITICAL DECISIONS.
BUT PUTTING THAT IN THE CONSTITUTION DIDN'T MAKE THE POWERFUL PEOPLE WANT TO LISTEN TO US.
A CONSTITUTION IS AN AGREEMENT, NOT A MAGIC SPELL.
FOREIGN INVESTMENT IS THE ECONOMY OF THE FUTURE!
THEY WANTED THEIR VERSION OF THE FUTURE...
EVEN IF IT DESTROYED OURS.
RAFAEL CORREA (PRESIDENT OF ECUADOR 2007–2017)

SO WHAT CAN WE DO?
WE KEEP STRUGGLING, USING THE TOOLS DEMOCRACY GIVES US:
PROTESTS, DEMONSTRATIONS, RESISTANCE
HOLDING THE POWERFUL ACCOUNTABLE EVERY TIME THEY BREAK THEIR PROMISES
ORGANIZING TO ELECT OUR OWN PEOPLE TO OFFICE
TALKING—TO EACH OTHER, TO THOSE WE DISAGREE WITH, TO PEOPLE WHO FORGOT WE HAVE A VOICE
FINDING COMPROMISES AGAIN AND AGAIN AND AGAIN
ECUADOR WILL ONLY BECOME TRULY PLURINATIONAL...
WHEN ALL THE NATIONS ARE TALKING *TO ONE ANOTHER* ABOUT A SHARED VISION OF THE FUTURE, ONE THAT INCLUDES EVERYONE.

DEMOCRACY IS CONSTANTLY CHANGING, ADAPTING, AND REINVENTING ITSELF FOR A NEW TIME OR PLACE.

BUT IT ALWAYS COMES BACK TO HAVING YOUR VOICE HEARD OR NOT.

WHO CAN PARTICIPATE, AND HOW, AND IF ALL CITIZENS ARE TREATED EQUALLY.

HOW CAN WE TRUST THE PROCESS IS LEGITIMATE IF WE CAN'T EVEN GET INTO THE ROOM?

HAVING A HEALTHY DEMOCRACY MEANS EVERY PERSON HAS THE TIME AND FREEDOM TO FIND THE WAYS THAT WORK BEST FOR THEM.

SO NEVER LET ANYBODY TELL YOU THERE'S ONLY ONE RIGHT WAY TO DO DEMOCRACY.

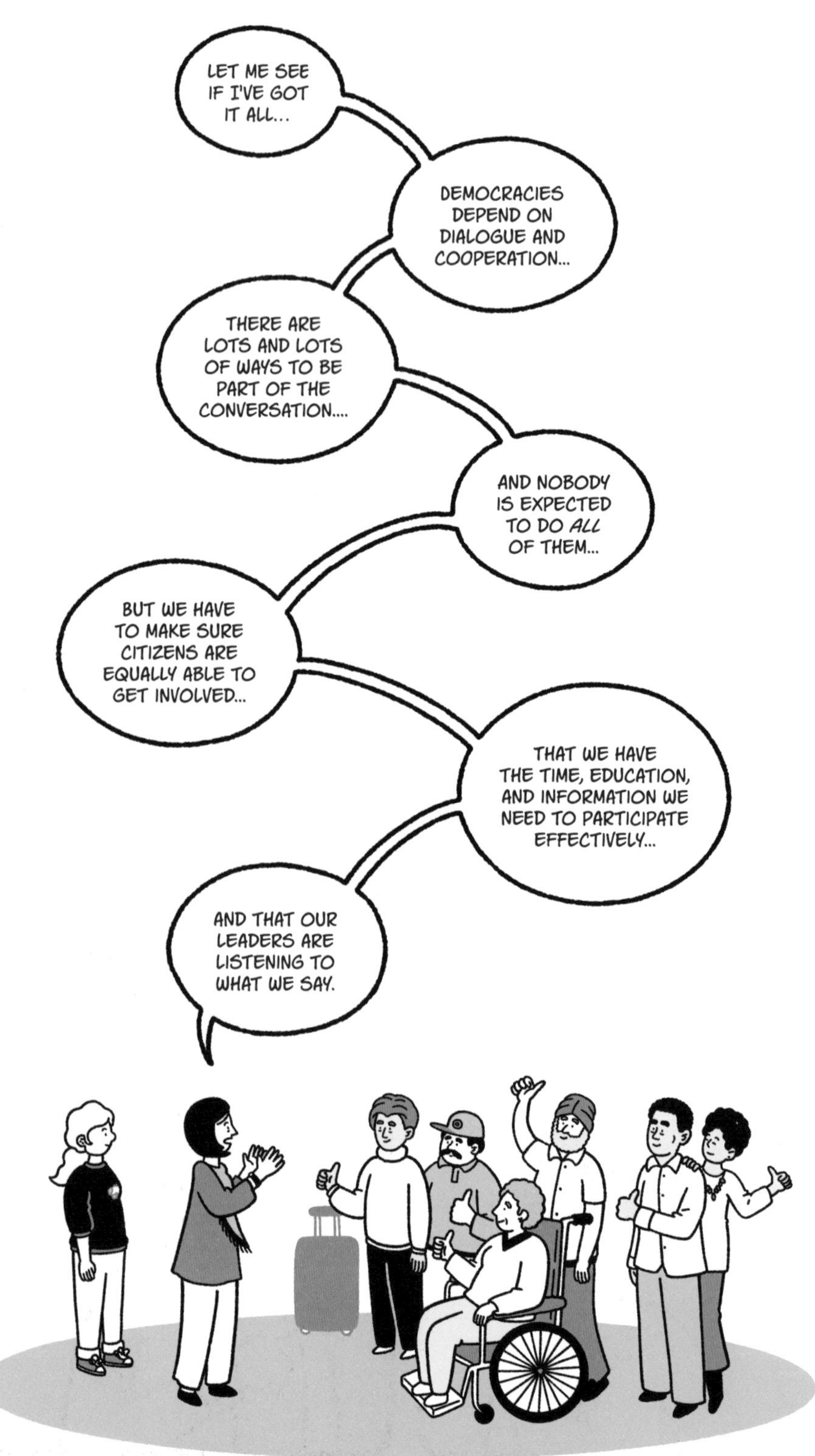

LET ME SEE IF I'VE GOT IT ALL...
DEMOCRACIES DEPEND ON DIALOGUE AND COOPERATION...
THERE ARE LOTS AND LOTS OF WAYS TO BE PART OF THE CONVERSATION....
AND NOBODY IS EXPECTED TO DO *ALL* OF THEM...
BUT WE HAVE TO MAKE SURE CITIZENS ARE EQUALLY ABLE TO GET INVOLVED...
THAT WE HAVE THE TIME, EDUCATION, AND INFORMATION WE NEED TO PARTICIPATE EFFECTIVELY...
AND THAT OUR LEADERS ARE LISTENING TO WHAT WE SAY.

WHAT DO YOU MEAN THE FLIGHT IS OVERBOOKED?
THIS IS THANKSGIVING! I HAVE TO BE ON THAT PLANE!

SIR, I PROMISE WE'RE DOING THE VERY BEST WE—
NO, I PAID FOR MY TICKET AND I WANT SOME ANSWERS! WHO'S RESPONSIBLE HERE?

I HOPE NONE OF US ARE SEATED NEXT TO HIM.
I DON'T UNDERSTAND PEOPLE LIKE THAT.
YELLING AT THAT WOMAN WON'T CHANGE ANYTHING.

THAT'S TRUE WHEN IT COMES TO AN AIRPLANE SEAT, BUT NOT WHEN IT COMES TO YOUR GOVERNMENT.

MAKING THE GOVERNMENT ANSWER FOR THEIR MISTAKES IS, LIKE, HALF OUR JOB AS CITIZENS.
THEY WORK FOR US, AND HAVE TO FOLLOW THE RULES, SAME AS ANYBODY.
IF THE RULES DON'T APPLY TO SOME FOLKS, THEN WE AREN'T REALLY EQUAL AFTER ALL.

NOT TO MENTION OUR LEADERS START THINKING ABOUT GOVERNMENT AS A WAY TO GET RICH, NOT SERVE THE PEOPLE.
LIKE THOSE ROBBER BARONS.
I HATE TO ADMIT IT, BUT ARISTOTLE WARNED US ABOUT THIS.
IT SOUNDS LIKE EQUAL TREATMENT IS KIND OF THE MOST IMPORTANT PRINCIPLE?
I AGREE. AND WE NEED TO BE HONEST ABOUT WHERE WE ARE NOW.
THERE IS PLENTY OF DISCRIMINATION IN OUR POLITICAL SYSTEM...
FROM THE WAY POLICE BEHAVE IN OUR STREETS TO WHOSE VOICE IS LOUDEST.
WE HAVEN'T MADE AS MUCH PROGRESS SINCE THE GILDED AGE AS I HOPED.
The color of your skin,
how recently you got here,
how much money you have...
DON'T FORGET GENDER. THAT'S A BIG ONE, TOO.
...it all still affects how you get treated by the government.

AND ALL THESE FACTORS CAN INTERSECT WITH ONE ANOTHER TO MAKE IT REALLY EASY TO GET YOUR VOICE HEARD...
...OR REALLY, REALLY HARD.
EVEN THOUGH WE STILL HAVE A LOT OF WORK TO DO...
DEMOCRACY STILL SEEMS LIKE AN IMPROVEMENT OVER THOSE OTHER GOVERNMENTS.
THEY DIDN'T SEEM TO CARE ABOUT EQUAL TREAMENT AT ALL.
I AM THE LAW AND THE LAW IS ME!
I WILL TELL YOU WHEN AND AGAINST WHOM THE LAW SHOULD BE USED.
BEING ABLE TO PUNISH MY ENEMIES IS JUST ONE OF THE MANY PERKS OF THIS JOB.
BUT I ALSO WORRY THAT DEMOCRACY IS MORE FRAGILE THAN I THOUGHT.
IT CAN BE.
LIKE IN ECUADOR. JUST BECAUSE THE PEOPLE HAVE THE POWER...
IT DOESN'T MEAN POWER ALWAYS SERVES THE PEOPLE'S NEEDS.

THAT REMINDS ME OF SOMETHING MY MOM LIKES TO TELL MY UNCLE.
IF YOU WANT THIS GOVERNMENT TO BELIEVE IN YOU, YOU HAVE TO BELIEVE IN IT!

DEMOCRACY HAS MANY ENEMIES.
THREATS TO DEMOCRACY
BAD ECONOMIES
WAR
CORRUPTION
OLIGARCHY
IF YOU SEE SOMETHING, SAY SOMETHING!
IT'S IN DANGER ANYTIME A LOT OF PEOPLE START THINKING "THIS SYSTEM ISN'T WORKING FOR ME."

OR WHEN SOME POPULIST STARTS SELLING THAT STORY FOR THEIR OWN ENDS.
HOLD ON...

IF THE SYSTEM ISN'T WORKING FOR A LOT OF PEOPLE, WE SHOULD DO SOMETHING ABOUT THAT!

SURE. BUT HAVEN'T YOU NOTICED THAT SOME POLITICIANS TALK ABOUT THE BROKEN SYSTEM ONLY WHEN THEY WANT MORE POWER?

THAT'S THE WHOLE POPULIST SCAM!

YEAH, THAT'S BASICALLY FUJIMORI IN PERU.

AND ONCE HE GOT INTO POWER, HE "FIXED" THE SYSTEM SO IT WOULD SERVE HIM AND HIS FRIENDS, NOT MOST OF THE PEOPLE WHO VOTED FOR HIM.

THAT'S POPULISTS FOR YOU.

HE USED REAL PROBLEMS TO MANIPULATE PEOPLE INTO GIVING HIM WHAT HE WANTED.

THE "PEOPLE" ARE VICTIMS OF CORRUPT ELITES
...AND "OUTSIDERS" WHO WANT TO TAKE WHAT THE "PEOPLE" HAVE.
REAL AMERICANS ARE BEING IGNORED—
FORTUNATELY, THE POPULIST HAS ALL THE ANSWERS.
BUT I WILL DRAIN THE SWAMP!
I AM NOT A CAREER POLITICIAN!
I CAN'T FIND A GOOD JOB!
GANGS ROAM OUR STREETS!
BUT HE WILL FIX THIS!
HE DOESN'T PLAY BY THEIR RULES!
IT SOUNDS GOOD TO FRIGHTENED, FRUSTRATED PEOPLE.
EXCEPT THE "RULES" HE WON'T PLAY BY ARE THE RULES OF DEMOCRACY.
← AUTHORITARIANISM
ALL OTHER GATES →
AND ONCE THEY'RE IN POWER, POPULISTS ALMOST ALWAYS TAKE AN AUTHORITARIAN TURN.

HOW DO YOU STOP THEM?
BY USING THE TOOLS DEMOCRACY GIVES US.

INCLUDE MANY PEOPLE IN DECISION-MAKING SO SOCIETAL GRIEVANCES DON'T FESTER.

USE OUR RIGHTS OF SPEECH AND ASSOCIATION TO MAKE SURE OPPOSING VOICES GET HEARD.
COMPLAINTS? SUBMIT HERE

GUARANTEE ACCESS TO INFORMATION AND EDUCATION TO UNDERSTAND WHAT IT MEANS.
INFORMATION
i

I ALWAYS THOUGHT THAT DEMOCRACY WAS A LITTLE LIKE TINKER BELL.

YOU KNOW, THE BLINKY FAIRY FROM PETER PAN.
WE GOT *THAT* PART.

IF YOU THINK DEMOCRATIC THOUGHTS YOU CAN FLY?
Y'ALL KNOW THAT PART WHERE TINK DIES...
NO, NO!
AND PETER PAN IS LIKE "CLAP CLAP IF YOU BELIEVE IN FAIRIES" AND IT WORKS?
I CLAPPED EVERY TIME EVEN THOUGH MY BROTHERS LAUGHED AT ME.
OKAY, SO IF YOU WANTED THE FAIRY TO LIVE YOU HAD TO BELIEVE IN HER **AND** YOU HAD TO DO SOMETHING TO SHOW IT.
SAME WITH DEMOCRACY.
YEAH, OKAY. YOU HAVE TO BELIEVE IN THE DEMOCRATIC CONSENSUS...
...AND THEN YOU HAVE TO SHOW IT BY PARTICIPATING IN THE PROCESSES THAT GIVE LIFE TO DEMOCRACY.
MY WORK HERE IS DONE.

I THINK WE ALSO PROTECT DEMOCRACY BY BEING HONEST ABOUT WHAT IT CAN AND CAN'T DO.
IT *CAN* DO A LOT OF REALLY GREAT THINGS.
WE WERE JUST TALKING ABOUT A BUNCH OF THEM.
UPHOLD OUR PRINCIPLES AND VALUES.
SOLVE PROBLEMS PEACEFULLY.
GIVE ALL KINDS OF PEOPLE A SAY IN THE DECISIONS THAT AFFECT OUR LIVES.
HOLD OUR LEADERS ACCOUNTABLE.
THERE'S A "BUT" COMING.
BUT IT CAN'T DO EVERYTHING.
DEMOCRACY DOESN'T AUTOMATICALLY MAKE EVERYBODY RICHER OR PULL EQUALITY OUTTA THIN AIR.
WE STILL GOTTA MAKE HARD DECISIONS ABOUT WHAT WE CAN DO WITH LIMITED RESOURCES.

DEMOCRACY DOESN'T EVEN KEEP ITSELF GOING.
WE GOTTA DO THAT.

IF WE EXPECT THE IMPOSSIBLE, WE'RE GONNA BE DISAPPOINTED AND MAYBE LOSE THE FAITH.
SO WE GOTTA BE HONEST WITH OURSELVES.

WE DON'T HAVE TO WAIT FOR A KING OR DICTATOR TO SOLVE OUR PROBLEMS, BUT THEY WON'T FIX THEMSELVES', EITHER.
THAT'S A GOOD POINT.
WE HAVE TO PUT IN THE WORK.

FLIGHT 5694 IS NOW BOARDING AT GATE 76.
THAT'S US!

WE GOTTA GO!
THANK YOU, EVERYONE!
I DON'T EVEN KNOW HOW MUCH I LEARNED.
WE CERTAINLY HAVE A LOT TO THINK ABOUT ON THE FLIGHT HOME!

TO MAIN CONCOURSE
WOW. THAT WAS QUITE A JOURNEY.
AND WE HAVEN'T EVEN LEFT THE AIRPORT YET!

WE ANSWERED QUESTIONS I DIDN'T EVEN KNOW HOW TO ASK.
AND SOMEHOW I STILL HAVE ABOUT A BILLION MORE.

WHAT ABOUT THE QUESTION YOU STARTED WITH?
ABOUT WHETHER DEMOCRACY REALLY IS SPECIAL?

HMM...I LIKE THAT IT GIVES EVERYBODY A VOICE. AT LEAST, WHEN IT WORKS RIGHT.
IT ALSO SEEMS MORE FLEXIBLE.
BUT...
BAD LEADERS OR LAWS CAN BE FIXED WITHOUT THROWING OUT THE WHOLE SYSTEM.

BUT?
DEMOCRACY ALSO SEEMS PRETTY FRAGILE.
I KEEP SEEING THINGS THAT BROKE IT.
WEALTHY PEOPLE USING GOVERNMENT TO STAY RICH.
GLOBAL TECH COMPANY PAYS $0 IN FEDERAL TAXES
POWERFUL PEOPLE AVOIDING ACCOUNTABILITY.
OFFICERS NOT INDICTED IN BRUTALITY CASE
POLLING PLACE
VOTE AQUI
POPULIST LEADERS UNDERMINING OUR BASIC RIGHTS.
POLLING PLACES CLOSED
LOTS OF FOLKS DON'T EVEN UNDERSTAND HOW GOVERNMENT IS SUPPOSED TO WORK IN THE FIRST PLACE.
YOU'RE RIGHT.
THE THINGS THAT MAKE DEMOCRACY SPECIAL CAN ALSO BE USED TO DESTROY IT.

AND WHAT COULD *I* DO TO SAVE IT?
I'M JUST A RECEPTIONIST AT A VET, I DON'T HAVE ANY POWER.
I HEAR YOU. I DON'T KNOW WHAT ONE WATER DISTRICT ADMINISTRATOR CAN DO, EITHER.
BUT THE POINT IS THAT WE DON'T HAVE TO DO IT ALONE, RIGHT?

THAT'S ANOTHER THING.
IT'S PRETTY CLEAR OUR DEMOCRACY WORKS A LOT BETTER FOR SOME PEOPLE THAN OTHERS.
HOW DO WE MAKE SURE IT WORKS FOR EVERYONE?
ALL GOVERNMENTS HAVE THEIR FLAWS, AND DEMOCRACY IS NO EXCEPTION.

I GUESS I'M WONDERING...
HOW DO WE GET FROM WHERE WE ARE TO A GOVERNMENT THAT LIVES UP TO ITS PROMISES?

Almost every country has ***basic*** government: protection from outside attackers, rules about what you can and can't do, and consequences for breaking them. But ***good*** government takes a lot more work.

The question is: Who is responsible for carrying that baggage, and are they willing to carry it?

EAGLE AIR

PREDICTABLE

TRANSPARENT

FAIR

ADAPTABLE

RESPONSIVE

INCLUSIVE

RESILIENT

REMEMBER WHAT ALL THOSE PHILOSOPHERS SAID GOVERNMENT IS FOR?
MAKING SURE WE LIVE THE RIGHT WAY SO WE CAN HAVE THE GOOD LIFE.

BUT THEY WERE WRONG! THERE ISN'T JUST ONE RIGHT WAY TO LIVE!
EXACTLY.

THAT MEANS WE HAVE TO ARGUE AND DEBATE...
AND TRY THINGS...
AND FAIL...
AND TRY NEW THINGS...
AND LISTEN TO WHAT OTHER PEOPLE THINK OF THEM.
DEMOCRACY IS THE ONLY KIND OF GOVERNMENT BUILT AROUND HAVING THESE CONVERSATIONS OVER AND OVER AND OVER.

SOME OF THE CONVERSATIONS HAPPEN ON BIG PLATFORMS.
BUT THEY ALSO HAPPEN IN TOWN HALLS AND IN THE COMMENTS SECTION OF THE NEWSPAPER...

AND EVEN IN THE AIRPORT WHEN ALL OUR FLIGHTS HOME ARE DELAYED!

WHEN OUR FAMILIES ARGUE ABOUT THE GOVERNMENT AROUND THE DINNER TABLE...
THEY'RE PART OF THAT CONVERSATION, TOO.

AND *THAT'S* WHAT SETS DEMOCRACY APART:
NOT JUST THAT WE'RE ALLOWED INTO THE CONVERSATION, BUT THAT WE'RE ESSENTIAL TO IT.

THOSE PHILOSOPHERS CAN KEEP THEIR PHILOSOPHER-KINGS AND PROPHET-LEGISLATORS AND VIRTUOUS RULERS!
THE GOOD LIFE HAPPENS WHEN WE WORK TOGETHER TO BUILD A GOVERNMENT THAT HAS A SEAT FOR ALL OF US...
THAT TRIES TO MEET ALL OUR NEEDS, AND THAT IS NEVER CLOSED TO GOOD IDEAS.
THE GOOD LIFE IS ALL OF US WORKING TOGETHER.

WHOO!
YEAH!
I'D VOTE FOR THAT LADY!
PREACH IT, SISTER!

It's not about finding the best government.

It's about building a government that does what's best for everyone it serves.

The best kind of government helps everyone get where they need to go.
AFTER YOU.
TICKET
END!

VOTE

author's note

Despite my ambitions when this project began, this book is not a comprehensive exploration of all the governments ever invented by human beings. Like any effort to cram an enormous topic into an accessible format, it is simplified in some places and incomplete in others. It does not, for instance, address supranational governance, parliamentary versus presidential democracy, or the many different forms of authoritarian rule. I have tried to provide a basic overview of the governments a reader is likely to encounter in the world today. If I have neglected your favorite government, please let my publishers know so they can ask me to write a second volume.

Readers may observe that this book does not discuss communist governments. This is because communism is an ideology that can inform government design, but it is not a form of government itself. Despite the claims of more than a century of propaganda, communism, socialism, and capitalism have neither inherent morality nor predetermined political futures. A country is no more destined for dictatorship if it adopts communist principles than it is destined for democracy if it adheres to capitalist ones.

Governance has a very simple question at its core: How can people solve problems and manage conflict? Three elements in this question shape everything that comes after. First, *people*: Who counts as a citizen, a decision-maker, a beneficiary, a member, a stakeholder, a human being? Government exists to serve the people, but until we know who "the people" are, we can't decide what kind of government will meet their needs. Second, *solving problems*: governments are expected to adopt laws, impose punishments, collect taxes, and do everything else they do to address real-life challenges. If a government is not solving (or preventing) problems for its citizens, then it is not performing its core function. Third, *managing conflict*: as this book makes clear, conflict is not an inherent problem for a society. But a government will lose both legitimacy and authority if people see violence as the best or only way to achieve their goals.

People solving problems to manage conflict; that's the seed planted at the heart of any government. How that seed develops depends on historical context, internal and external influences, resource constraints, and the stories we tell about who we are and who we want to be. There is never only one way to build a democracy, a monarchy, a dictatorship, etc., etc., . . . just as no one person ever has all the answers to society's problems.

So: This book is an incomplete record, governments are both fundamentally simple and infuriatingly complex, and nobody has one correct final answer. In the end, all an author is left with is hope.

It is my hope that readers gain a basic understanding of how governments work, as well as curiosity about the context and history that shape governments around the world. I hope you come away with renewed enthusiasm to fight for governments that are responsive, predictable, transparent, fair, inclusive, adaptable, and resilient. I hope you know your government needs your voice and I hope you believe, like Lin, that the good life comes from all of us working together to meet the challenges of our times.

EAT IN
TAKE OUT

the GOVERNMENT *bistro*

a quick reference

OPEN
24 / 7

Starters

Start your Government Bistro experience here!

LEGITIMACY

Citizens believe officials are using their power appropriately and according to established rules.

Packed with essential nutrients for a growing government!

AUTHORITY

Citizens accept that the government has power to make rules and enforce them.

You can't say no to this one!

Main Courses

Choose one or mix and match to make your favorite combo!

MONARCHY

One person is the supreme head of government and rules for life. Law and custom dictate how power is transferred, but it is usually hereditary.

Now in two flavors!

Absolute monarchy

Supreme lawmaking power, can hire and fire senior government officials, and is not accountable to any other part of the government.

Constitutional monarchy

The symbolic leader of the nation. Retains some powers, but most government functions are held by leaders chosen according to a constitution.

DICTATORSHIP

For the discerning customer who wants it all, government revolves around one person and operates to keep them in power. Comes with a side of secret police and your choice of intimidation or control of the media.

Absolutely no substitutions.

ARISTOCRACY

Decision-making power is restricted to a small group connected by kinship, bloodlines, and landownership. A good choice for traditional diners.

Perfect for the big spender looking for more!

OLIGARCHY

Extremely wealthy people control most government decisions, even if they aren't officially in government. Treat yourself, make your friends jealous, and keep everybody else away from the table!

THEOCRACY

Feel righteous about your choice! Government based on religious laws and principles, where most important decisions are made by members of the clergy. Can be served in a bowl or wrapped in the trappings of secular government.

WARLORDISM

Fight off your rivals at our all-you-can-eat buffet. Enjoy absolute decision-making power as long as you maintain superior military strength and control economic leverage points.

DEMOCRACY

There's something for every adult citizen to love, because every adult citizen gets a say in how it's made! Equality under the law is flavored with universal suffrage and free expression.*

Choose from among our exciting flavor combinations: liberal, social, direct, representative, deliberative, participatory, plurinational, or make your own!

**Substitutions available whenever leaders fail to keep their promises.*

Add to any of our main courses to give them extra zing or send them in a new direction!

Populism

Shake up the system with an outsider who claims to speak for the unheard majority. Pairs well with dictatorship, whether you want it to or not.

Patronage Politics

Keep everyone coming back for more with an irresistible combo of cushy government jobs, luxury items, and essentials for survival!

Democratic Consensus

No matter how you dress up your democracy, people won't be satisfied without widespread belief in democratic principles.

A staple for any functioning democracy!

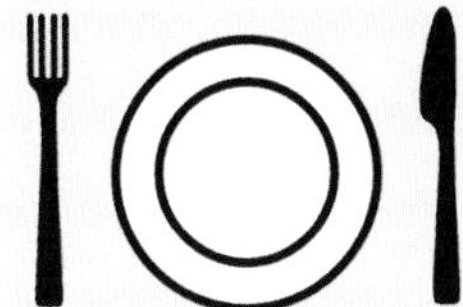

acknowledgments

Just like governments, a book is the product of many people working together to achieve what seems, at times, like an impossible goal. I am grateful to many people for their work on this project, particularly Ally Shwed, a true partner whose artistic genius makes even the driest topics compelling to read. I am additionally grateful to Mark Siegel, Samia Fakih, Kirk Benshoff, Alexander Lu, Angelica Busanet, and the rest of the team at First Second, who brought this book to life and created the wonderful series of which it is part.

I owe a deep debt of gratitude to Aparna Polavarapu, Lil Taiz, Mohammed Al-Shuwaiter, Nikki Mandell, Valerie Turner, Wang Zheng, and others unnamed here for generously donating their time and expertise. This book is more accurate and more interesting because of their contributions, and any errors of fact are mine alone. Thank you also to Allison Grossman, Shawna Burke, Ryder Cobean, and Whitney Edmunds Swann for reading drafts and for constant encouragement. I appreciate you pretending that my government jokes are funny.

And to my wife, Chelsea, an endlessly supportive partner who read every word and knew when it was time to stop rewriting. I can never thank you enough.

—Beka Feathers

First, my endless thanks to Beka, for being the mastermind behind this book and deeming my illustrations worthy of conveying her ideas; and to Mark Siegel, for believing in me and in the power of comics to effect change in the world. To the entire First Second team, including Samia Fakih, Kirk Benshoff, Robyn Chapman, Alex Lu, and Sunny Lee, thank you for lending your talents, skills, suggestions, and support to make this project achieve its highest potential. To my family and friends, for their constant encouragement and unyielding support, and, of course, to Gerardo, my favorite cartoonist.

—Ally Shwed

Beka Feathers is a legal adviser on political development in conflict-affected states. Her writing is influenced by her work with clients and partners in more than a dozen countries, where she has helped to draft constitutions, design transitional governments, facilitate peace processes, and advocate for improved access to justice. She lives with her talented, pun-loving wife and a suspiciously intelligent dog in Portland, Oregon.

Ally Shwed is a cartoonist, writer, and editor. She received her MFA in sequential art from the Savannah College of Art and Design and has worked with the *Boston Globe*, the *Nib*, *Topic Magazine*, and the *Intercept*. Together with her partner, artist Gerardo Alba, she runs Little Red Bird Press, a visual arts studio specializing in comics and printmaking. Her other recent projects include the graphic novel adaptation of *Fault Lines in the Constitution* (First Second Books) and *Votes for Women*, a comic anthology about the Nineteenth Amendment (Little Red Bird Press). She currently lives in Los Angeles, California, with Gerardo and their two cats, Egon and Schneider.

further reading

ABOUT DEMOCRACY:

How Democracies Die, Steven Levitsky and Daniel Ziblatt, Crown (2018).

Of the People, By the People: A New History of Democracy, Roger Osborne, Bodley Head (2011).

On Democracy, Robert Dahl, 2nd ed., Yale University Press (2015).

On Democracy, E. B. White, Harper (2019).

HISTORY:

Fujimori's Peru: Deception in the Public Sphere, Catherine M. Conaghan, University of Pittsburgh Press (2006).

The History of the Standard Oil Company, Ida M. Tarbell, McClure, Phillips & Company (1904).

The Making of Asian America: A History, Ericka Lee, Simon & Schuster (2016).

The Republic for Which It Stands: The United States During Reconstruction and the Gilded Age, 1865–1896, Richard White, Oxford University Press (2017).

The Second Founding: How the Civil War and Reconstruction Remade the Constitution, Eric Foner, W. W. Norton & Company (2019).

State of Blood: The Inside Story of Idi Amin, Henry Kyemba, Putnam Publishing Group (1977).

You Are Not American: Citizenship Stripping from Dred Scott to the Dreamers, Amanda Frost, Beacon Press (2021).

PHILOSOPHICAL FOUNDATIONS:

Al-Farabi on the Perfect State, Al-Farabi, translated by Richard Walzer, Oxford University Press (1985).

Mencius, Mencius, translated by D. C. Lau, revised ed., Penguin Classics (1970).

The Muqaddimah, Ibn Khaldun, translated by Franz Rosenthal, abridged and edited by N. J. Dawood, Princeton University Press (2005).

Politics, Aristotle, translated by Benjamin Jowett, Batoche Books (1999).

ONLINE RESOURCES:

"Democracy," Max Roser, Our World in Data, https://ourworldindata.org/democracy (2013).

Participo: Research and Practice of Innovative Citizen Participation, OECD, https://medium.com/participo.

Stanford Encyclopedia of Philosophy, https://plato.stanford.edu/index.html.

Published by First Second
First Second is an imprint of Roaring Brook Press,
a division of Holtzbrinck Publishing Holdings Limited Partnership
120 Broadway, New York, NY 10271
firstsecondbooks.com

Library of Congress Cataloging-in-Publication Data is available.

First edition, 2022
Edited by Mark Siegel and Samia Fakih
Cover design by Kirk Benshoff
Interior book design by Sunny Lee and Angela Boyle
Color by Gerardo Alba Rojas
History consultant: Valerie Turner
Authenticity reader: Alex Lu

Special thanks to Angelica Busanet

Penciled and inked with Kyle's blot blot brush (modified) in Adobe Photoshop.
Digitally lettered and colored in Photoshop.

Printed in Singapore

ISBN 978-1-250-76070-8
1 3 5 7 9 10 8 6 4 2